Humor in the Court

By Larry Siegel

Attorney at Law (Retired)

Contents

Introduction

This book is about ordinary people confronting their legal challenges in small town rural America. The author, Larry Siegel, draws upon his forty-six years of experience as a practicing attorney in rural Walla Walla, Washington, bringing to life the humorous side of his clients' serious legal issues.

A small-town attorney must deal with a wide variety of legal matters compared to the big city attorney who often specializes in one unique area of the law. In rural areas, there is an expectation by clients that their attorney, who may belong to their service club, church, or country club, will take care of whatever legal issue arises. The client who signed a will yesterday may need a divorce tomorrow, have a son who got a drunk driving citation over the weekend, or is selling his business next week.

It all adds up to the small-town attorney wearing many hats when it comes to the diverse legal issues that arise on a daily basis. While virtually all of the cases have an amusing side to them, along the way the reader is rewarded with many useful legal nuggets that are instructive in understanding and navigating our challenging legal system.

Lawyers routinely prepare disclaimers to protect their clients from liability from those who utilize their goods, services and advice. Information presented in this book is not intended to be the last word on the legal issues discussed. Laws change over time and no two situations are identical. Accordingly, the reader of this book should consult with his/her own attorney when addressing issues similar to those presented herein, including but not limited to, this discussion of disclaimers.

The names of the individuals appearing in this book have been changed to preserve their anonymity.

1

The Bimbo Clause

As a young attorney, I found myself drafting lots of wills for family members and acquaintances. Like most attorneys, I relied on basic will forms that I had placed on my computer. I filled in the blanks with the names while adjusting the language to accommodate the idiosyncrasies of each client. Everyone's situation was a little different which required personalizing the will to fit the circumstances. It was rare when a client did not disclose some unique circumstances such as children from a prior marriage, a child with special needs, or a child who was completely estranged. Even with a standard long term conventional marriage with two natural children, there was often a need for special terms.

Andrea and John Alston, who had two children and four grandchildren, appeared to be the perfect fit for my standard will form known among estate planning attorneys as an "I love you will." In this format, each spouse leaves everything to the other spouse, and upon the death of the second spouse, everything is distributed equally among their children.

"I want a bimbo clause in my will," Andrea Alston announced, as her husband John looked on in silence. Andrea, in her early 50's, had a short blond page boy haircut, bright red lipstick, and matching fingernail polish. John was tanned with a full head of salt and pepper hair. On this warm sunny day, he was dressed in navy blue Bermuda shorts and a lime green polo shirt. Without question, Andrea was the driver and John the passenger in this consultation with their attorney.

"What is a bimbo clause? Never heard of that one," I confessed.

"You know," Andrea explained. "I die and leave everything to John. John remarries some bimbo and changes his will to leave everything to the bimbo. John then dies and our entire estate goes to a bimbo I have never met. Our kids get nothing. I want an ironclad provision placed in our wills that totally prevents that disaster from happening."

There was a pause. I glanced at John who was not making eye contact and then back at Andrea. "Let me see if I can translate what you want into legal terms," I offered. "What I think you want in your wills is the creation of a Trust upon the passing of the first spouse. The surviving spouse will receive income from the Trust assets for life. Then, upon the death of the surviving spouse, the Trust assets will go to your kids. The unknown bimbo has no claim to the Trust assets or involvement with the Trust," I concluded.

"That's just what I want. A bimbo clause!" Andrea emphasized as John studied my framed law degree hanging on the wall behind me. Andrea did have a valid point. The fact pattern she described where the bimbo inherits everything is a real possibility if a surviving spouse fails to take the necessary precautions to protect the children. I had just never heard of this precautionary language termed a "bimbo clause" before.

"I know what you want," I said looking at Andrea. "I suggest I prepare drafts of your wills for the two of you to review. You can write questions and changes directly on the will drafts. Make sure I have all the names spelled correctly. Based upon your input, I'll then make modifications for your final review before you sign. My secretary will notify you when the drafts are ready. You can either pick up the drafts or we can email them to you so that you can print them off for review. Sound good?" I concluded.

"Sounds like a plan," Andrea replied. "I'll leave my cell phone number with your secretary on the way out. She can give me a call when the drafts are ready for me to pick up. Thank you for seeing us," Andrea said as she and John stood up. John quickly shook my hand without saying a word. As the couple departed, John turned and quickly provided me with his first real communication of our meeting, a prodigious eye roll that said it all from his perspective.

As I placed the Alstons' file on my ever-growing "pending" stack on the credenza behind my desk, I had the distinct feeling that I would come to learn the history behind Andrea's unique request for a bimbo clause in her will.

2

Counting Crimes

Criminal Law 101: Final Exam   Number: 348

The crime scene:

Mack and Al were leaving the locked house through the ground-floor window they had jimmied open. Moonlight reflected off the flat-screen TV that Al was carrying. Mack had a box of sterling silver tucked under his left arm.

Owen Owner, hearing the noise from upstairs, leaned out his bedroom window and screamed, "Stop or I'll shoot!" whereupon Gil Getaway, standing on the street by his Camaro, opened fire and shot Owen between the eyes, killing him instantly.

Hearing the shots, Ned Neighbor called 911 and hid under his bed. Al and Mack ran across Owen's yard and leaped into Gil's waiting Camaro. The Camaro took off at a high rate of speed, sideswiping Ned's parked car as they pulled onto the street. The police, with sirens blaring, gave chase to the getaway car. The Camaro, squealing around a corner, struck a drunk walking in the crosswalk, killing him instantly. Spinning out of control, the Camaro smashed into some garbage cans and skidded to a halt as the police closed in from all sides.

A shootout ensued. One police officer shot and killed another officer who was approaching from the opposite direction. After Gil was wounded in the stomach, all three, Gil, Mack, and Al, raised their hands and surrendered.

Explain in detail what crimes were committed.

Almost on cue, the sound of piercing sirens began blaring outside the law school. One after another, the wail of the sirens rose and then fell as the emergency vehicles raced down Winter Street.

Oh my God! This is crazy, I thought. Sound effects accompanying the final exam in Criminal Law! As if I'm not already totally stressed out. Gotta focus and block out all the outside noise.

Carefully rereading the description of the crime scene, I began jotting down notes as I gathered my thoughts.

Mack and Al are guilty of a burglary, I typed. Oh, I better throw in the requirement that for it to be a burglary under the Common Law, the entry into the home must have been in the nighttime which it clearly was, given the mention of the moonlight.

I continued typing. Gil Getaway, who never entered the house, is nevertheless guilty of burglary also because he is an accomplice. Under the law, accomplices are just as guilty as the principal who commits the crime. Since Gil shot Owen Owner and killed him, Gil is guilty of murder. Although neither Al nor Mack fired a shot, they are also guilty of murder under the Felony Murder Rule which provides that all of the parties involved in a felony are fully accountable for any murder that a co-felon commits due to the great danger attendant to the commission of any felony.

All three, Mack, Al and Gil, can be charged with malicious destruction of property for the damage caused to Ned Neighbor's car as they pulled away from Owen's house, as well as for damage to the garbage cans which they crashed into at the end of the chase, using the same reasoning regarding accomplices. Normally, Gil would be guilty of negligent homicide of the drunk killed in the crosswalk since he was the driver. However, since this homicide happened during the escape from a felony, the charge is raised to murder under the Felony Murder Rule. Also, since Al and Mack are accomplices, they can be held responsible for the murder of the drunk as well. Accomplices are held accountable for every crime committed by the principal, in this case, Gil. Mack, Al and Gil can all be charged with murder for the death of the police officer also even though none of them fired the shot that killed him. The Felony Murder Rule applies to all participants in a felony even though they were not the direct cause of death.

I'm running out of time, I thought as I glanced at my watch which I had placed on the table next to the exam. The two hours had flown by.

Charge all three with eluding a police officer, I typed just as the whistle shrieked, announcing the end of the exam.

I wrote my law school exam number 348 on top of my exam and handed it to the proctor standing at the door. To avoid the slightest suggestion of impropriety in the grading process, we were not to write our names on the exams. Instead, we wrote our designated exam number on the front of the test. The professor grading the exam would then write our numerical grade by our exam number. After Christmas vacation, our grades for all five classes were to be posted on the bulletin board in the lobby. No names would appear. Just our exam number.

As I stepped into the wood-paneled high-ceilinged law school lobby, the voice level was deafening. One hundred forty-two emotionally stressed law students were talking at once. With no prior exams or grades during the entire four-month semester, we had all been swimming in the same tense sea of uncertainty. The questions we were asking ourselves were, where do I stand in this class? Does that guy next to me understand this stuff better than I? Does that woman who always sits in the front row really know the material better than the rest of us? She seems to have all the answers when a professor asks a question. When we began the semester in August, our first-year class totaled 164. As we prepared for final exams in December, the number of students in our class had dwindled to 142, the attrition the result of a Darwinian selection process that weeded out those unable or unwilling to cope with the unique stresses and challenges of law school.

Locating a group of my friends, I joined them in celebrating the completion of our first law school exam. We had four more tests to go before Christmas vacation, but at the moment they were of little consequence. Together we had slogged through the semester and survived that first exam, an achievement for the moment worth savoring.

Six days later, just having finished the last of the five exams, Contracts, it was time to drive home for the holidays. The seemingly endless semester had been the most grueling and academically challenging experience of my life. During my four years of college at the University of Washington I lived in a fraternity where I always had roommates and lots of friends around. In addition to attention to studies, I attended football games, enjoyed social events with my girlfriend, Claire, and generally had a well-rounded college life. So different from my isolated law school experience this past semester.

As I began college, Pre-Med sounded like a good major (my dad was a doctor), but a C in chemistry, an allergy to formaldehyde, as well as a generally poor performance my first quarter, quickly derailed that plan. It did not take a genius to conclude that studying in the fraternity house was an unmitigated disaster. Too many distractions such as card games, ping pong, billiards and the ever-present pranks.

By the second quarter, I had discovered the quiet majesty of Suzzallo Library, the awe-inspiring Gothic campus "cathedral." The calm solitude of the study carrels located on the third floor of Suzzallo became my home away from home, at least during weeknights. With improved study habits, my grades rapidly improved. By spring quarter of my senior year, I received notification that I was admitted to Phi Beta Kappa, a national academic honorary which honors graduating seniors who are in the top 10% of their class. Armed with a solid resume, I began exploring graduate schools but had no specific plan.

During the final quarter of my senior year, I decided, without much enthusiasm, that law school would be a good option, so I took the LSAT test (law school entrance exam) and applied to four or five schools. One slight problem. When I finally submitted the applications in May, I was too late to be admitted for classes in the fall. In early June, as I was reviewing job options, I received a pleasant surprise in the mail. I had been accepted for the fall semester as a late admittee to Willamette Law School, a solid small private school located in Salem, Oregon, adjacent to the state capital grounds. With no other attractive options, I decided to give law school a try.

Knowing no one at Willamette, I rented an unfurnished apartment in Salem and, at age 22, began living solo for the first time in my life. As evidence of my lack of long-term commitment, my little apartment remained unfurnished for the duration of the semester. Unfurnished, that is, except for a mattress on the floor in the bedroom and a card table and chairs obtained from Goodwill that I placed in the kitchen. I had no television and never acquired any living room furniture. In keeping with my minimalist décor, I hung a Pacific Railroad calendar on the kitchen wall to the right of the sink. I could have easily vacated the entire apartment in less than fifteen minutes.

Commencing August 18th when classes started, I began an evening ritual which I continued until the end of the semester in December. Each evening at 11:00 pm, as I finished studying at my card table, I stepped to the calendar and with a large black sharpie, I ceremoniously made a king-sized X over the day just completed. I was a prisoner, one day closer to the end of my sentence. I was committed to giving law school my best effort, but the first semester was not to be the happiest time in my life.

3

Red Light or Green Light?

Having just completed my fifth and last final exam in Contracts, the interminable first semester of law school had finally concluded. It was mid-December with snowflakes drifting down past my kitchen window as I locked my apartment to begin the five-hour drive home from Salem to Walla Walla. First I would pass through Portland, then along the Columbia River Gorge to Hood River and continue east along the Columbia River for another three hours to Walla Walla. Traveling alone, I had plenty of time to think about my future.

With no grades the entire semester, my final exam results were to be my only objective measure of success. Considering the expense and the stress, did I really want to continue with law school if I did not get positive feedback from the final exam results? The test results were not going to be posted until after Christmas vacation in January.

Looking back on the semester, I was confident I had given my best shot at determining if this were to be the career path I would pursue. As I fell into a rhythm of attending classes and studying, my competitive instincts had kicked in. Once I had begun to grasp the legal terminology, it all started to make some sense. The legal profession truly does have a language all its own. Since mid-August, when the semester began, I estimated my efforts included devoting approximately 90 hours a week to law school between studying and attending classes. I did, however, make an effort to get in some physical exercise every day.

Glancing to my left out the car window at water rushing over The Dalles Dam, I made my decision. My exam results were going to be the litmus test as to whether or not I continued with law school and a legal career. With the effort required, the stress level, and the financial investment, I needed a clear signal that I was good at this before I continued with law school for another two and a half years. There were plenty of other interesting and financially rewarding careers out there that were far less demanding.

Sharing time with Claire and my family, visiting friends, and doing some skiing, Christmas vacation flew by quickly. The six-hour drive back to school along the icy Oregon gorge was agonizingly slow. It was already dark when I arrived in Salem at 4:40 PM. The lit up three-story brick law school building appeared especially foreboding that evening. My heart was pounding as I prepared to learn which direction my life would take.

A cluster of students was gathered around the bulletin board perusing their exam results. I had a sudden urge to pee and quickly darted into the men's room. As I was standing at the urinal, I noticed some fresh graffiti on the wall facing me. ARNOLD IS AN ASSHOLE someone had printed in bold black letters with a sharpie pen. Not up to the usual law school graffiti standards, I thought, while making the assumption that the author must have received a disastrous test score in Torts from Professor Arnold. After slowly washing my hands, I made my way out to the lobby to face the music.

By now there were only three other students scouting out their test scores posted on the bulletin board. It suddenly struck me that a side benefit to the anonymity provided by the use of exam numbers rather than individual names was embarrassment avoidance. None of my classmates need know if I were a complete failure. Popping a Rolaid into my mouth, I began the search for number 348.

Number 348 must be here somewhere. Let's see. Civil Procedure. OK. Not a disaster. There is one down. Oh, there is Number 348 again. Oh, I did better than I expected in Contracts. This is looking good so far. Oh, and I did really well in Torts. As I searched for my Criminal Law test score, the memory of all those sirens during the exam came flooding back to me. Wow! Criminal Law came out just fine too. And how about that! One of the top grades in Real Property. Well, son of a bitch! This is outstanding! Looks like I am going to be around this place for a while.

Driving home the following weekend, I was on a high. All my effort over the past four months had paid off! Time to celebrate a little and bring two long forgotten friends to law school..... my tennis racquet and my golf clubs. I might even find a roommate who owns a television for this coming semester.

4

A Nearly Perfect Interview

Claire and I were married in our home town of Walla Walla, Washington the summer after my lonely first year of law school. We had lived off her teacher's salary through my third year until graduation.

Having just received word that I passed the two-day rigorous Washington bar exam, I was fully licensed to practice law. Whew! What a relief! But now I needed to find a job. Since Claire resigned her teaching position last June, we had no income. With the goal of settling in the Seattle area, we set up camp in Claire's sister and brother-in -law's semi-finished basement in West Seattle. We were not paying rent as my job search continued, so we were always looking for odd jobs around their home as our contribution.

Our latest project was refurbishing their floor-to-ceiling brick fireplace which their predecessor had painted an unfortunate solid seafoam green.

"I'm just not a good job seeker," I announced as I finished the last chapter of The Firm by John Grisham.

"You have a great resume. Something good will develop." Claire was reassuring me. "But you have to get out there and knock on some doors."

It was much easier to send out letters to law firms while enclosing a copy of my resume. My letters always ended with a request for an interview. This approach allowed me to lie on the couch reading novels while I waited for law firms to contact me. After all, my resume confirmed that I had graduated from college with honors and finished near the top of my law class. To create an air of respectability, I had shaved off my mustache and had my hair cut short for my professionally generated photo that appeared at the top of my resume.

After rejection following two interviews with well known downtown Seattle law firms, I was reluctant to put my ego on the line again. "You have an impressive resume, but we are not hiring at this time." I rationalized that it was a tight job market for attorneys. The big firms hired from within the ranks of those law students who had clerked for their firms prior to graduation. The clerkships were the firms' pipeline for future associate hires. In other words, virtually all of the attorney associate positions with the most desirable firms were already filled by the time I got my act together.

Despite having a terrible cold, I decided to keep the scheduled interview with Dean Kegley, a partner in the firm of Winston and Mortimer with offices on the 23rd floor of a chrome and glass office building in downtown Seattle. Upon entering Mr. Kegley's office, I quickly took in the spectacular floor to ceiling sweeping view of Puget Sound and made my way straight to the client's chair across from Mr. Kegley's gigantic mahogany desk. In his late thirties, with slightly receding curly red hair, Dean, as he asked me to call him, was the type of guy you couldn't help but like. Wearing grey slacks, an obviously expensive white shirt and navy-blue tie, Dean smiled frequently and made me feel comfortable from the outset of the interview.

Having many common interests, we talked more about golf and tennis than lawyering. Discovering that we had a mutual acquaintance famous for his drinking exploits, we exchanged stories about our entertaining friend, Bob Burkenstein. We then went on to trade "Bob stories." Dean laughed uproariously when I described our inebriated friend, with opened umbrella, ala Mary Poppins, jumping out of my second story apartment window. Bob survived the fall with just a few scrapes and bruises, the favorable result most likely a product of his relaxed condition.

Dean followed my "Bob story" with one of his own. While attending a Saturday night bachelor party on the eve of his friend's wedding, Bob had plunged off the diving board into an empty swimming pool. Again, miraculously no lasting injuries. However, extensive black and blue bruising to Bob's face caused him to forego attendance as a groomsman at the wedding the next day.

Sensing rapport growing with my interviewer, I tried one more story about the time Bob launched his golf bag and clubs into the lake by the 18th green following completion of his round with his foursome. The group was back at the clubhouse in The Grill Room before Bob realized his car keys were tucked away in his golf bag that was resting at the bottom of the lake.

Observing Dean checking the time on his gold Rolex, I determined it prudent to end the story there rather than dragging it out by detailing Bob's exploits in retrieving his keys. Good decision to cut it short, I thought, feeling very positive about how Dean and I had hit it off during the interview.

"That's quite a story," Dean chortled. "Hey, this really has been great, but I'm overdue to see a client. You mentioned you heard from Bob recently. Can I get you to write down his contact information for me? I heard he and his wife just had a baby. I probably should send them a note or a baby gift or something," Dean said as he handed me his fancy black desk pen together with a yellow notepad. He placed his left hand on the corner of the notepad to keep it from sliding. I had become so absorbed in the conversation that I had completely forgotten my miserable cold. As I leaned over to begin writing, to my horror, my nose dripped a copious amount of snot that fell squarely on the back of Dean's freckled left hand. The largest viscous glob had splatted all over his gold wedding band. "Sorry about that," was all I could muster, completely mortified.

As I fumbled clumsily through my pockets for a Kleenex, Dean quickly pulled out a DK monogrammed handkerchief. Carefully wiping away the nasty wet debris from the back of his hand, in a voice dripping with sarcasm, he concluded the interview with, "You really ended the interview on a high note!"

Mr. Kegley did not call me back the next day or ever.

5

The Two Martini Job Offer

I was standing at the bathroom sink just starting to shave when I got a phone call.

"I just got a great job with a big personal injury law firm in Tacoma," my law school buddy, Pat Darnold, gushed.

"That's great," I said wiping a dab of shaving cream off my phone. I was making an effort to sound enthusiastic while fighting back pangs of envy.

"But that's not the reason why I called," he continued. "When this job offer came along, I had a lead on another opening in Redmond with a three-man firm. The youngest partner is leaving. They are looking for a replacement." With my niece's red crayon, I jotted down the firm name on the back of an old envelope. I thanked Pat profusely for the lead and wished him good luck in his new job.

Redmond is a fast-growing Seattle suburb just east of Lake Washington. Located near a busy intersection, the one-story law office was in a strip mall between a beauty parlor and an osteopath. A Shell gas station was just across the street.

As I sat in the waiting room of Cantrell Law Offices that Wednesday morning, I had visions of my nose drip fiasco that had effectively harpooned my last job interview. Fortunately, I was over my cold. Not going to make that mistake again.

Mr. Cantrell, the senior partner, was approximately 40 years old. He was friendly but talked so much I hardly had a chance to say a word. His office had no windows, deep red shag carpet, cedar paneling, and a fireplace at the end of the spacious room. To the left of the fireplace was a wet bar. Behind Mr. Cantrell's large desk was his commitment to being casual. Inexpertly applied to the wall was an 8x10 foot billboard sized 7-Up poster. Not unlike having a pop machine in the oval office, I thought as I attempted to keep a straight face.

"I see you made law review," Mr. Cantrell complimented me, glancing down at my resume. After about 30 minutes of chatting (I avoided telling any golf stories), we adjourned to the Crossroads Restaurant for a sandwich. "Would you care for a drink?" he inquired. I started to decline, but recalling the bar in his office, I concluded that my host must be a fairly active drinker.

"Oh, why not?" I responded. "What are you going to have?"

"I'll have my usual vodka martini with one olive," Mr. Cantrell said to the cute cocktail waitress.

"Make that two of them," I said. "I mean the same for me, not two olives," I explained to the waitress who was not amused.

After a sandwich and a second martini, we were back in Mr. Cantrell's office. "I think you would be a good fit here," he told me as he offered me a position as an associate in his firm. My ego indicator was spinning out of control. I actually had a job offer! Trying to remain calm, I told Mr. Cantrell I was flattered by the offer, the two martinis adding to my euphoria.

Fighting the reflex action to say, “I'll take it,” my mind began racing. Instead, I heard myself saying, “That's exciting. Would it be possible for me to have two or three days to think this over before I make a final decision? Can I get back to you on Monday?”

“Monday would be fine,” he replied as I stood up and pumped his hand.

Claire was just putting the finishing touches on our fireplace project when I returned. She was covering up the seafoam green with brick red paint. My job was to apply beige colored paint filling in the spaces between the bricks to give the appearance of mortar.

“Congratulations!” Claire said enthusiastically after I proudly announced the job offer. “That's awesome! But you need to be sure it's the position you want to take.”

“Well, Cantrell did say I could have two or three days to think it over,” I replied slipping into my painter's clothes, old jeans and a faded purple University of Washington sweatshirt. “Why don't we go home to Walla Walla and take one final look to see if there's a decent opening there? We've run out of places to paint around here anyway. Then on Monday, I can call Cantrell and tell him I'll take the offer.”

No surprise, it was pouring rain as we crossed the Bellevue floating bridge, the gigantic University of Washington Husky Stadium looming to our left behind us in the low clouds. We drove on past Bellevue and Issaquah. The I-90 freeway over Snoqualmie Pass was icy, making travel slow and treacherous. Halfway across the state in Vantage on the Columbia River, the wind was blowing an icy 40 m.p.h. but at least there was no snow. The remainder of the trip along the river and through the deserts of Central Washington and the Tri-Cities was relatively easy. We arrived in Walla Walla a little over five and a half hours after having left Seattle.

"Larry, I just may have something for ya," Dirk Montana was saying to me over the phone in his low booming voice. Dirk, who had been practicing law in Walla Walla for fourteen years, had been a family friend since his high school football days.

"Jerry Blumenthal is leaving the Prosecutor's Office and they've got to be looking for someone," Dirk continued. "I don't see any reason why you wouldn't be perfect for the deputy prosecutor job. As a deputy prosecuting attorney, you're allowed to do civil work as well as prosecute criminal cases. That means you can start a private practice doing wills and divorces in addition to prosecuting criminals for the state. You'll be in court a ton. If you think you'd be interested, I'll call up Art Eggerson, the head prosecutor, and set up a meeting for you."

"Claire, this just could be it! I can have a private practice too."

"What are you talking about?" she said looking up from her thick novel.

"The Prosecutor's office may have an opening. I think one of the deputies is leaving. In addition to prosecuting criminals, I can do private civil work there, too, like wills, divorces, and personal injuries."

"It all sounds great but maybe you should wait until you at least have an interview before you get too excited," she cautioned. "After all, Mr. Cantrell is still waiting for you." It was no secret, she preferred living in the more metropolitan Seattle area, having attended the University of Washington for four years. We had lots of college friends residing in Seattle and Claire's grandparents lived on Vashon Island, just a twenty-minute ferry ride from West Seattle. Perhaps the choice would be made for us. If no opportunity were to arise in Walla Walla, I was going to accept Cantrell's offer in Redmond.

6
Walla Walla

With a population of around 40,000 folks, Walla Walla, Washington is a farming community that spreads out lazily at the base of the Blue Mountains in the southeastern corner of the state of Washington. Located just 6 miles from the Oregon border, its repetitive Native American Nez Perce name means "Place of Many Waters." Walla Walla is known for its rich surrounding wheat lands, sweet onions, Whitman College, and the Washington State Penitentiary. Walla Walla is also the birthplace and childhood home of the original Batman, otherwise known as Adam West. Each autumn Walla Walla hosts an annual Adam West Day featuring the Batmobile and Bat copter.

Most recently, the Walla Walla Valley has become internationally known for its burgeoning wine industry. With an enology and viticulture program at the local community college, there are now more than 140 wineries in the valley. Main Street is lined with wine tasting rooms, upscale restaurants, and fancy tourist shops. On the outskirts of town, bright green vineyards adorn the hillsides. Despite the influence of the wine industry and the local colleges, Walla Walla remains primarily a farming community. The pickup trucks still far outnumber the Mercedes, BMWs and Range Rovers.

Montana had arranged for me to be interviewed by Arthur Eggerson, the current prosecuting attorney for Walla Walla, Washington. "Everyone just calls him Art," Dirk had advised me. The Prosecutor's offices were located on an upper floor above Drumheller's Hardware Store in a 75-year-old brick building that was in dire need of remodeling.

The Drumheller building's rickety elevator was personally operated by an elderly, silver-haired, bespectacled lady who was wearing a printed name tag on her short sleeved white blouse. The name tag announced that she was HELEN. Pulling down on the metal lever, Helen caused the massive elevator door to slide shut behind me. Next, she pulled down on a second lever which made the rickety elevator lurch several times, jiggling the loose milky white skin hanging from her upper arms. A final lurch, and we started our slow and shaky ascent as Helen began speaking.

When the lighted number above the elevator door indicated that we had arrived at the 4th floor, I prepared to exit. Not so fast. Helen was making no attempt to open the door. I was a captive audience as she proudly continued her story, detailing her 10-year-old granddaughter's soccer heroics from last evening. With great pride, Helen described the winning goal Jessica scored in the last minute of the game. Signaling my urgency to move along, I glanced repeatedly at my watch, but I was going nowhere. At last, Helen finished her story and only then did she pull down the lever to open the door, allowing me to make my escape. I made a quick mental note for future reference. Always take the stairs when visiting the Drumheller building.

Three doors down on my left, a beige door with a frosted glass window announced "OFFICE OF THE PROSECUTING ATTORNEY" in large black print. No frills at the taxpayers' expense, I thought, as I surveyed the spartan appearance of the fourth floor that housed the Prosecutor's office.

Before entering the office, I turned the corner and continued down the dark hallway to the men's room. I wanted to make certain I had no black seeds between my teeth and that my necktie knot was not askew. The restroom walls were enormous slabs of white and grey marble, no doubt quite expensive back in the day. Placed across one of the two floor- to-ceiling urinals, a giant pipe wrench held a square piece of brown cardboard in place. On the piece of cardboard, the janitor had printed in bold black ink, "Out of Order." Just below his inscription, in a different handwriting, someone had scrawled "Since 1942."

Arthur R. Eggerson had held the position of Prosecuting Attorney for Walla Walla County for the past 22 years. Dressed in a gray and white pin striped suit and black tie, Mr. Eggerson was a large man of approximately 6 feet 3 inches in height. His wavy gray and black hair defied direction.

"I remember refereeing a high school football game you played in a few years back," Mr. Eggerson said with a smile as he pumped my hand. "Everyone just calls me Art," he said as he continued. Art spoke in partial sentences, leaving it for the listener to complete the thought. "Not like the big city law firms here," he said. "Not stuck in the law library doing research all day. Court room right away," he muttered reaching out to accept a letter from his secretary, Jo Ann. Art's speech could not keep up with the rapid functioning of his brain. Art's eyes darted across the page. He reminds me a little of Don Quixote in a three-piece suit, I thought as he dashed out of the room. Was the interview over?

Forty-five seconds later he was back. "Can you start the first of next month?" he asked. "Gotta run.... Court house... Court. Running late. Jo Ann! ... the Martin file... I'll blast those bushers right out of the ballpark!" Art proclaimed to no one in particular as he rushed out of the office.

Ignoring the elevator, Art raced down the four flights of stairs, leaving me asking myself, what just happened? I think I just got a job offer. In the equation, my academic performance was clearly a distant second in importance to my exploits in a football game years ago. I was pretty sure Art did little more than glance at my resume that had taken me three arduous years to build. Most likely he did ask around among the attorneys in town who knew me. It was my good fortune. There was a job opening and here I was. Right place at the right time. I owed Dirk Montana a big thank you.

Assuming I was taking the job, Jo Ann handed me the paperwork I needed to fill out to come aboard. Rather than accept the position, I told Jo Ann I would need to talk it over with my wife and get back to her. "Hope Art didn't need these papers in court that he left behind on my desk," she chuckled as I said my goodbyes.

The quick transition from no job offers in sight, to two at the same time, was a little mind boggling. Although I knew Claire's preference was to live in Seattle where most of our college friends had settled, the Prosecutor's office in Walla Walla promised to be an excellent opportunity to get my feet wet in a hurry. The job would come with lots of immediate court room experience as well as provide an opportunity for me to lay a foundation for a private practice. Claire had taught three years in Oregon and it turned out there was a need for elementary school teachers in Walla Walla. With these job opportunities, it ended up being an easy decision. I took the job offer at the Prosecutor's office while Claire accepted a position as a 4th grade teacher at Green Park Elementary. Suddenly we were both very much a part of the establishment, settling down in Walla Walla, Washington to begin careers in education and the law. Back in my hometown, I was feeling more comfortable with the familiar surroundings, slower pace and, yes, drier climate.

7
Learning the Ropes

While in many states criminal prosecutions are pursued by District Attorneys, in the state of Washington we are referred to as Prosecuting Attorneys. All thirty-nine counties in Washington elect their own Prosecuting Attorney who hires deputies, all licensed attorneys, to assist with pursuing criminal charges against the perpetrators. Prosecutors are granted authority to initiate criminal charges by filing a sworn statement called an Affidavit of Probable Cause, which sets forth facts confirming that a crime has been committed, which then must be approved by a judge.

Including myself, there were three deputy prosecutors in the office, all working for Arthur R. Eggerson, Prosecuting Attorney, in and for the State of Washington, County of Walla Walla. The older senior deputy, Carl Hanson, a thoughtful cerebral type, handled mostly civil cases that involved such matters as zoning and county planning. The other deputy prosecutor was the feisty bull dog, John Griggs, Chief Criminal Deputy. John prosecuted both adult felony cases and juvenile matters. Initially, I would begin by prosecuting the small-time crooks and traffic offenders in the lower District Court. However, I was assured that I would soon be handling the more serious felony cases in Superior Court.

In addition to having authority to file charges for crimes committed, prosecutors in Washington state also have discretionary powers to plea bargain as well as dismiss charges. Imbued with these powers, as if by magic, I was transformed over night from a poor student jobseeker to a power broker with control over people's lives. Silver-haired defense attorneys in three-piece suits were approaching me for concessions on behalf of their clients. I began hearing requests that went something like this. "If you will reduce the felony charge to a gross misdemeanor, I can get my client to plead guilty with no need for a trial."

Another common refrain went something like this. "My client has been a solid citizen and a productive member of the community for 25 years. Other than this one mistake, his record is spotless. He is most deserving of leniency." Soon police officers and deputy sheriffs were requesting direction from me regarding the sufficiency of their search warrants and propriety of their arrest procedures. Newspapers and radio stations were asking me for quotes about newsworthy crimes.

While law school had trained me to distinguish between an assault, a burglary and a robbery, I was learning on the job the procedural tightrope a prosecutor must successfully traverse to avoid destroying the investigative efforts of law enforcement. The treatise titled The Rules of Evidence became my bible. In addition to all the procedural rules, I knew nothing of the practical problems that confront a prosecutor with a heavy caseload. Do we go to trial or accept a plea to a lesser charge and thereby avoid the expense of trial and uncertainty of a jury decision? I was just beginning to learn about time priorities, plea bargaining and expense factors as well as jury and witness unpredictability. Because of all these considerations, most criminal cases do not go to trial. If my case against a defendant were strong, typically he or she would plead guilty to one of several charges on condition that I dismiss the other charges. The plea bargain generally included my sentencing recommendations as well. For example, the defendant charged with first degree assault would plead guilty to second degree assault if I would recommend to the judge that he serve only six months in jail. With a guilty plea, I then had a conviction without the time and monetary expense of a trial and an uncertain result with a jury.

There was a benefit to charging as many crimes as I could find from the facts presented, much like my law school final exam in Criminal Law. For example, if a man grabbed a purse off a lady's shoulder and ran, but was later apprehended, I would charge him with assault, theft and robbery. If the case were strong, his attorney would contact me to discuss a plea bargain that would lead to his client pleading guilty to one or more of the charges on dismissal of the others. I would estimate that over ninety percent of the criminal cases were resolved in this manner.

My first few months in the Prosecutor's office consisted of learning the ropes as to court room procedures, getting acquainted with the judges and court personnel, the clerks, the bailiffs, the court reporters, meeting the local attorneys, and making decisions on a daily basis that affected people's lives. No one was telling me how to do it. It was trial by fire. I made some mistakes but learned from them.

Virtually everything and everyone was new to me. I was totally drained by the time I got home each weekday evening, but I was quickly gaining valuable courtroom experience that I would call upon for the rest of my legal career.

8

Citizen's Arrest

Having been in the Prosecutor's office all of two weeks, I was busy Monday morning determining what charges to file against weekend offenders based upon the facts set forth in the stack of police reports sitting on my desk. Each typed police report prepared by the arresting officer set forth facts which told a story that typically translated into one or more crimes defined under the Washington Criminal Code. My task was very similar to answering the question presented on the law school final exam for Criminal Law: *What crimes were committed?*

Most of the action took place on Friday and Saturday nights. Felonies with stiffer penalties were filed in Superior Court while misdemeanors and traffic citations were heard in District Court. As a newbie in the office, I was assigned the unenviable task of prosecuting misdemeanors and traffic citations in District Court on behalf of my client, the State of Washington.

Before taking over as the prosecutor in traffic court, I had one afternoon of training which consisted of my attending court as an observer while seated at the Prosecutor's table next to Carl Hanson, the pipe smoking seasoned Deputy Prosecutor in his late sixties. One after another, for more than two hours, the accused offenders paraded before Judge Martonick to answer the charges filed against them. The offenses ranged from speeding tickets, to possession of marijuana, to drunk driving citations. Most defendants pleaded guilty with an explanation while hoping for a reduced fine.

If the defendant pleaded not guilty, a brief trial was held on the spot. To prove the state's case, Carl called the arresting officer as his witness. Carl asked the officer questions that produced the necessary testimony to convict the defendant. He always asked if the activity occurred in Walla Walla County which established the court's jurisdiction over the matter. Judge Martonick often interrupted to ask pertinent questions that the prosecutor may have overlooked. Perhaps questionable procedure, but small-town justice that seemed to work. That afternoon only one defendant was found not guilty when the judge ruled that the state had not met its burden of proof on a drunk driving charge, determining that the breathalyzer machine had not been properly calibrated. As my on-the-job court room education continued over the next several months, Carl's advice and observations would prove to be invaluable.

Before I could finish reading the first police report on my desk that Monday morning, I was interrupted by my secretary on the intercom. "There's a Mr. Harrison Marshall on the phone. He says he made a citizen's arrest over the weekend regarding a drunk driver. Good luck!"

I picked up the receiver, punched down on the lighted button, and heard Harrison Marshall speak for the first time. "I want to press charges on that drunk driver last Friday night," he began.

"I haven't received that police report yet," I confessed, burning my tongue on the hot coffee. "It usually takes a day or two before the police department delivers their reports up to the prosecutor's office. But since you're on the phone, why don't you explain what happened and I'll read the police report when I receive it."

"Sounds fair to me," replied Marshall, and launched into his tale. "Well, I was traveling up toward Walla Walla from Milton-Freewater, Oregon about sunset. I was still on State Route 125 just past Walmart headed north for town when this guy we were following crosses the center line and forces this oncoming car onto the shoulder. The guy in front of me continued driving erratically, slowing way down and then speeding up. He crossed the center line several times. People were honking at him and shaking their fists, but he continued down the road as if nothing had happened. Too bad no police around. Seeing how he very nearly killed some people, I decided to follow him and not let him get away with this. He drove into town and through some side streets, through neighborhoods, but I was able to keep up with him even though it was getting pretty dark."

Barely catching his breath, Marshall continued. "Well, he drove downtown, pulled into the dark alley behind McFeeley's Tavern and stopped his car there right in the alley. I parked real fast out on 4th street, ran into the alley, and found him there standing next to his car, drunker than a skunk."

"This is getting interesting," I understated, taking another sip of my coffee.

He continued, “So then I collared the drunken S.O.B. and told the bum we were going to the police station.”

“What did he say?” I asked, chuckling to myself.

“He says, anything you shay mishter! He was slurring his words. Had trouble walking the three blocks to the police station, staggered a lot, but seemed pretty happy the whole time. I marched him into the police station, told the officer at the front desk what happened, and that I wanted to file charges for drunk driving. Another officer came out of the back room and took the guy away to give him a breath test, I guess.”

“Did you fill out a written statement?” I inquired.

“Yes. I filled out and signed a statement describing the situation. The officer told me the drunk’s name is Wallace Aycock or Hitchcock or something like that. Just before I left, they told me the guy had a .16 or 1.6 percent alcohol on that machine that measures alcohol. Anyway, I hear that’s plenty over the drunk level. The officer told me that if I want the guy charged, to give the prosecutor a call Monday morning. For some reason, the officer said he couldn’t give the guy a ticket on the spot, but that you probably would. The officer gave me your name and phone number."

"The reason the officer couldn't give him a ticket is that he didn't observe the offense committed in his actual presence," I explained authoritatively, while hoping I was correct. "When a police officer issues a citation for drunk driving typically the officer has personally observed the offense. As an eyewitness, the officer is authorized to give a citation based upon the officer's personal observations and investigation. Following a citizen's arrest, the prosecutor must sign an Affidavit of Probable Cause that the crime was committed. Considering what you've told me on the phone now, I see no problem with prosecuting this case but first I'll need to read the police report. Assuming that the officer's report confirms your narrative, I'll complete the affidavit and file it with the court. I'll then send a Summons to the driver to appear in court to face the charge of Driving Under the Influence of Alcohol. My office will confirm the trial date with you by mail. I'll need you as a witness in case Mr. Babcock pleads not guilty. And thanks for all your help," I concluded.

Five days later, I wrote the following letter to my prosecuting witness, Mr. Harrison Marshall:

Re: State v. Wallace Andrew Babcock

Dear Mr. Harrison Marshall,

Having reviewed the police report, I have now formally charged Wallace Andrew Babcock with Driving Under the Influence of Alcohol (DUI) in Walla Walla County, State of Washington. The case is set for trial on August 8th at 2 p.m. in District Court located at 6th and Poplar Streets in Walla Walla, Washington. I will need you as an eyewitness to the drunk driving charges. Please notify me immediately if this date is unworkable for you. Otherwise, I will assume you will be present at the court hearing to testify if the defendant should plead not guilty.

I will meet with you at the Clerk's office located adjacent to the courtroom about 1:30 p.m. on August 8th to review your testimony with you. You should be aware that there is a possibility that Mr. Babcock may not appear for the court date, in which event the judge will issue a bench warrant for his arrest. If Mr. Babcock pleads not guilty, I will call you as a witness for the state. I will ask you questions so that you may tell the judge what you observed. The officer who gave Mr. Babcock the breathalyzer will also be a witness. As the court docket is rather lengthy, you may have to wait a few minutes for the case to be called.

In advance, we thank you for the time and cooperation you are affording the state in this matter.

Very Truly Yours,

Larry Siegel

Deputy Prosecuting Attorney,

Walla Walla County, State of Washington

Because they are so rare, no one in the office had any particular insights as to how to prosecute a citizen's arrest case. I did, however, learn that police officers frown upon citizens' arrest cases because the training and experience that law enforcement officers bring to the crime scene is completely absent, creating a much greater likelihood that the case will not hold up in court.

There is a subtle distinction in play, however, when a citizen makes an arrest. Constitutional protections such as the 4th amendment precluding unreasonable searches apply solely to actions by the state (police), but not to actions by individuals interacting with each other. For example, if a police officer has a search warrant for your neighbor's home and mistakenly enters your home and finds cocaine, the evidence is inadmissible because it violates the 4th amendment against unreasonable searches. The police officer, acting on behalf of the state, has no legal right to be in your home and therefore no probable cause for the search. However, if your neighbor finds cocaine in your home while watering your plants in your absence and turns the cocaine over to the police, the evidence is admissible because the constitutional protection against unreasonable searches applies exclusively to state action.

9

Directing Traffic

It was my maiden voyage serving as the prosecuting attorney in traffic court. In my navy-blue suit, white button-down shirt and navy and white striped tie, my place was at the prosecutor's table on the right side of the courtroom facing the judge. Seated on several rows of wooden benches behind me was a mishmash of local characters in court to answer to their various traffic tickets and misdemeanor offenses. Many of the defendants had brought along friends and relatives to lend moral support, swelling the group to roughly seventy-five in the small windowless court room. Having observed court last Friday, I knew that most of the defendants would plead guilty while hoping for a reduced fine. Those who pleaded not guilty would have a brief trial on the spot, Judge Martonick presiding. Those demanding a jury would have their trial set for a later date.

To my right, half a dozen blue uniformed state troopers sat shoulder to shoulder on a wooden bench against the wall. The troopers, impressive in their crisp blue uniforms and shiny silver badges, held their navy blue Smokey the Bear hats in their laps. The troopers were available to testify as witnesses should any defendant have the audacity to plead not guilty to a speeding ticket, drunk driving citation, or other traffic offense. The people behind me chatted among themselves as a baby cried from someone's lap.

From the hallway the portly Judge Martonick entered, his black robe flowing. There was no formal bailiff or court reporter, and thus no formal record of the proceedings. One of the police officers bellowed, "All rise!" The entire group in the courtroom rose as one, and suddenly it became quiet as everyone watched the 6'3", 260-pound judge lumber up the two steps and seat himself in the leather high backed chair behind the lectern.

"Ladies and gentlemen, please be seated," Judge Martonick announced, while scowling at the foot high stack of tickets in front of him. It was exactly 2:00

p.m. No way we will be finished by 5:00 p.m. I thought, glancing at the crowded room behind me.

In an authoritative voice, the judge announced the format in his court. "As your name is called, please step forward and the charges will be read. You may plead guilty, guilty with an explanation, or not guilty. If you plead not guilty and the arresting officer is present, a brief trial will be held if that is your desire."

Next the judge began calling the names alphabetically, peeling each citation from the top of the stack. "Ernest Adams." He repeated the name while scanning the audience for Mr. Adams, but no one stepped forward. "I'll issue a bench warrant for his arrest," the judge growled in the direction of the troopers. "Failure to appear in court on a summons."

Meting out rapid fire justice, Judge Martonick continued to whittle down the stack of tickets in front of him. He found most all of them guilty while providing each defendant with the opportunity to explain the ever-present extenuating circumstances. Carl had mentioned that this being an election year, the judge generally reduced the stated fine on the ticket by as much as fifty percent. Most folks left pleased with the outcome as well as with a much greater likelihood that they would vote for this wise and friendly judge next fall. Virtually everyone was given a carrot for bothering to show up.

Judge Martonick, not known for his foreign linguistic skills, announced the case of State versus Aurelio Gustavo Gutiérrez, while impartially butchering each of Aurelio's three hispanic names. A few muffled chuckles quickly stopped when the judge glowered at the audience. As Mr. Gutiérrez and his court appointed interpreter stood before the bench, the judge inquired of Mr. Gutiérrez in a friendly voice, "How do you pronounce your name, anyway?"

"Geelty," came the quick response from Mr. Gutiérrez triggering raucous laughter in the crowded court room. Even the normally expressionless state troopers were cracking up. Judge Martonick pounded his gavel while demanding silence. Poor Aurelio, who spoke no English, had been instructed to say "guilty" following the first question asked of him by the judge. Offering a begrudging smile, Judge Martonick accepted the guilty plea, reduced the fine, and suspended jail time.

"State versus Wallace Andrew Babcock," the judge announced my citizen's arrest case. I had already confirmed that my witness, Harrison Marshall, was in attendance, waiting patiently in the back of the court room. Officer Jillian, who had performed the breathalyzer test on Mr. Babcock, was also present. Would Babcock show up for the trial? If he did appear, would he plead guilty thereby relieving me of the stress of trying a citizen's arrest case in front of a full courtroom? The state troopers and police officers were getting their first impression of me, the young neophyte prosecutor. I could feel the perspiration moistening my armpits.

Wallace Babcock was a white male in his fifties, red faced with two days growth of salt and pepper beard and receding gray hair. Wearing a brown and beige checkered flannel shirt, Mr. Babcock held a sweat stained crimson and gray Washington State Cougar ball cap in his hands as he stood before the judge. "Please plead guilty," I said a little prayer to myself.

"Not guilty, your honor," Babcock quietly announced his plea to the charges.

Damn it, I thought while announcing in my most authoritative voice, "The state calls Harrison Marshall." It was up to the state to put on its case first. I had to at least act like I knew what I was doing!

My first witness, Mr. Marshall, quickly came forward from the back of the court room. Armed with notes affixed to his clipboard, Marshall was wearing a three-piece dark blue polyester suit, white button-down shirt and black tie. Reading his notes through his black horned rimmed glasses, Mr. Marshall eloquently but laboriously repeated the story he had told me on the phone, almost word for word. The attentive audience chuckled when he came to the part about dragging the defendant from the alley behind McFeeley's tavern to the police station. When asked to identify the person he had taken to the police station, Mr. Marshall pointed his finger directly at Babcock seated at the table to my left. "That's the guy," Marshall stated dramatically.

Next, Officer Jillian stepped forward. In response to my questioning, Officer Jillian explained the results of the breathalyzer test that confirmed Babcock's drunken condition. "What personal observations of the defendant did you make at the time you gave him the breathalyzer," I asked. The officer stated that Mr. Babcock had slurred his words, staggered when he tried to walk, and was clearly intoxicated.

"The state rests, Your Honor," I announced in a loud and confident voice.

"O.K. Mr. Babcock," the judge stated, "You may now tell your side of the story. Step forward please and I will swear you in as a witness."

The onlookers shifted in their seats to get a better view of the defendant. Now seated in the witness chair, Babcock squinted at the large audience in front of him. After swearing to tell the truth, Babcock spoke to the judge. "My apologies, Judge," he said in a soft voice. "I ain't never been through this sort of thing before. You're gonna hafta tell me what I'm s'pose ta do."

"You need to state your full name and then just tell your side of the incident," the judge informed him, glancing at the clock and back to the still large stack of tickets.

"My name is Wallace Andrew Babcock," the defendant began in a halting voice as he twisted his hands back and forth in his lap. "Mostly they call me Wally," he explained. "Well, on July 22, I think that was a Friday, me and Roy was drinking beer all afternoon at McFeeley's Tavern. 'Bout dark, I guess it must have been, uh, 'bout 8:00 o'clock, I headed to the back to use the men's room but the door was locked." He paused to catch his breath. "I remember I couldn't wait any longer. Had to go really bad so I went out the back door to the alley to take a .... relieve myself. There was this car in the alley parked right by the back door. I just finished taking a leak next to the car when this wild man comes running up into the alley and says he's gonna take me to the police station. I'd just come out of the bright lights from the tavern. Still couldn't see no good. The guy was excited 'bout something and I wasn't objecting to no one in that dark alley, s'pecially with my pants still unzipped." He paused again and I sneaked a look at the judge who was tapping his pencil on the stack of citations that remained in front of him.

"Guess I wasn't feelin no pain neither as that there breath machine tells you," he continued. "Do know that I put down a lot of beer that day. I showed up today because I ain't so sure what crime I committed. Wasn't drivin' no car. Don't even own a car so how can I be charged with drunk driving? Guess that 'bout sums it up," he concluded. Perspiration glistened on his forehead as he pushed himself up from the witness chair while placing his baseball cap back on his head.

Not bothering to see if the prosecutor might ask him a question or two on cross examination (I had none), Wally pointed to someone seated near the back of the room. "I brought a witness," he said as he stepped down from the witness chair. Forward sauntered Roy, who turned out to be Wally's drinking buddy. With roadmap eyes, spotty beard, and dark greasy hair, Roy made Wally look reputable.

"Everything Wally says is true," Roy began. "Sep't I ain't so sure of the exact time. Didn't see what happened in the alley neither. Kinda lost track of time that night, I guess. But I was drinking with Wally at McFeeley's all that afternoon and evening. Wally said he was going to take a leak. Oh, sorry, I mean relieve himself. I never saw him again that night. Not sure what happened to him. And I got stuck with the bar tab," Roy concluded amid laughter from the attentive audience. Not waiting for me to ask him any questions on cross examination either (I had none), Roy stepped down.

Even a rookie prosecutor in traffic court knows that he must prove two elements of a drunk driving charge to obtain a conviction. First, he must show that the defendant was drunk. Secondly, he must prove that the defendant was, in fact, the driver of the motor vehicle. While I had proven drunkenness beyond any reasonable doubt, it was obvious I had a serious problem proving the identity of the driver.

The judge looked down at me and in a barely audible voice asked, "Did anyone obtain the registration off the car in the alley?" Obviously, the judge was fishing for a way to link Babcock to the vehicle. I glanced to my right at Officer Jillian who was now seated by the wall, and noticed he was shaking his head from side to side indicating the answer was no. Mr. Marshall, my eye witness, was doing the same behind me.

"No, Your Honor," I responded to the judge.

"Mr. Babcock," announced Judge Martonick, "your story is so unbelievable that I am going to believe it! Case dismissed," barked the judge, shaking his head. There were chuckles from the state troopers who seemed quite satisfied with the conclusion to my ill-fated citizen's arrest case.

Wally and Roy left the courtroom together, soon to be toasting their victory at their usual table at McFeeley's, no doubt. With clipboard in hand, Harrison Marshall departed the court room out the back door without speaking to me. That was an unmitigated disaster I thought. But my humiliation was brief as the judge quickly moved on to the next case.

By 3:45 pm, Judge Martonick had plowed through roughly two-thirds of the citations, having reached the P's. He called the case of State versus Roland Plumley, a truck driver who was cited for transporting a load in excess of the weight allowed by law. Trucks are limited by weight depending on the number of their axles and other factors I did not fully understand.

Truck drivers must stop at weigh scales along interstates where their vehicles are weighed. The fine may be considerable if the vehicle's weight exceeds the legal limit.

Scanning the citation without looking up, the judge announced, "Mr. Plumley, you are charged with being overweight. How do you plead?" All was quiet for a moment. Then as the rotund Mr. Plumley lumbered forward to stand in front of the judge, the visual began to sink in among the onlookers. When someone from the back of the court room snickered, the flood gates were opened to uproarious laughter, causing the judge to hammer his gavel repeatedly while demanding quiet. The red-faced Mr. Plumley quickly pleaded guilty to "being overweight," whereupon the judge cut his fine in half.

I jotted r*es ipsa loquitur* on my yellow legal pad next to the name Roland Plumley, recalling the Latin phrase we learned in law school. Translated into English the phrase means, "The thing speaks for itself."

Finally, at 4:50 pm Judge Martonick had heard the last case on the docket. The court room was now deserted except for the judge and me. I was packing up my files, exhausted from the stress of my first day as a prosecutor in traffic court.

"How about that citizen's arrest case?" Judge Martonick remarked as he walked by on his way to his chambers. "That was the craziest set of facts I've ever heard."

"Not a great outcome for the prosecutor," I replied. "But if I ever write a book, that case will be in it."

10
Where In the World Is Winston?

Police Report

Location of Occurrence: Sears Department Store in Walla Walla, Washington.

Suspect: Westerweller, Winston W.

Sex: Male

Ethnicity: African-American

Age: 27 years

Height 5'11"

Weight: 147

Arresting Officer: Detective Lyle Adams

Description of Offense: White male suspect was seen by a store clerk "acting furtively" near the back of the hardware section in

Sears Department Store. The clerk continued to observe suspect and watched suspect exit back of store via rear door pushing a rototiller ahead of him. Clerk exited back door of Sears in pursuit of suspect and observed suspect pushing rototiller east down the alley behind Sears. Clerk apprehended suspect in alley. Rototiller recovered. Detective Adams called in to investigate. Suspect arrested by Detective Adams, taken to Walla Walla Police Department where booked for 2nd degree theft (the value of the stolen property was less than $750). Suspect very friendly but refused to give statement. Handwritten statement of Sears clerk attached to this report. Rototiller held in evidence locker at the Walla Walla Police Department pending trial.

Arresting Officer's Comments: Suspect dressed in white clothing from head to foot. His mind does not focus well.

Later that morning, Detective Adams stopped by my office confirming that there really was a person legally named Winston W. Westerweller. Detective Lyle Adams, approximately 40 years of age, was a plain clothes police detective who took his job seriously. On that warm spring afternoon, the detective wore polished brown cowboy boots, beige slacks and a short-sleeved white dress shirt. His bolo tie was cinched up tightly at the neck with a shiny black agate.

Finding no humor in the situation, the earnest Detective Adams gave me the lowdown on Winston W. Westerweller. Winston, formerly known as Derek Smith, the detective advised me, had come to Walla Walla from Chicago where he had been involved in a barroom brawl while playing pool in a tavern. During the altercation, Derek took a blow to the head from the fat end of a cue stick, knocking him out cold. When he regained consciousness, Derek began acting differently in several respects.

Following his release from the hospital, Derek had his name legally changed to Winston W. Westerweller. He purchased a new wardrobe, decking himself out from head to toe in pure white. He began ignoring the need to pay for items he removed from stores. And finally, in keeping with his new "W" fixation, Winston bought a bus ticket to Walla Walla, Washington. Upon his arrival in Walla Walla, Winston rented an apartment on West Willow Street. Winston's good fortune continued as he quickly landed a job as a window washer at Whitman College.

"You gotta be making this up," I told the detective.

"I am giving you the facts as best I know them," Detective Adams replied without the slightest hint of a smile.

Winston appeared in the crowded courtroom to face the theft charges dressed in his solid white uniform; white shoes, white slacks, white shirt as well as white gloves, all in striking contrast to the many checkered flannel shirts and faded denim jeans seated on the wooden benches around him. Prior to his court appearance, I had made a plea deal with Winston's court appointed attorney, a guilty plea in exchange for suspending all but 7 days of jail time.

Following Winston's guilty plea and my recommendation, the black-robed Judge Martonick peered down from the bench at Winston through his half-framed glasses while stating matter of factly, "Mr. Westerweller, I'm going to sentence you to 90 days in jail, but I'll suspend all but seven of those days. You'll do one week in jail." Thereupon a heavyset deputy sheriff stepped forward to escort Winston out of the courtroom to the county jail.

Shortly after Winston's one week stay in the county jail, Detective Adams was back in my office dropping off a new police report detailing another crime involving Westerweller. This time Winston was caught shoplifting a white dinner jacket from Sporleder's, a local men's clothing store. "Must've been invited to a formal gathering," I commented to the detective who did not smile at my effort at humor.

In court two days later, Winston was sporting his trademark white outfit but with one addition. This time he was wearing white noise cancelling headphones clamped over his head completely covering his ears, which, together with the remainder of his stark white outfit, gave him the appearance of a Martian from outer space. I saw no sign of the white dinner jacket he had lifted from Sporleder's, most likely having been stored in an evidence locker at the police station.

Once again, Winston was pleading guilty, this time based upon my willingness to recommend to the judge that he receive a reduced sentence of 10 days in jail. With the sheer number of defendants parading before him in his court, Judge Martonick might occasionally overlook a prior offense when considering sentencing. However, in Winston's case, there was no forgetting him. Ignoring my recommendation, Judge Martonick sentenced Winston to 30 days in jail.

Following his month in jail, on several occasions, I saw the white clad Winston pushing a shopping cart up and down the sidewalks of Main Street. The shopping cart was loaded with magazines and other assorted accoutrements- fans, blenders, clothing and food items. How he obtained these items, and the nature of his mission as he pushed the cart up and down sidewalks, was a mystery. But given Winston's penchant for acquiring goods sans payment, it was only a matter of time before we would meet in court again.

11

A Tale of Whoa

As I became more comfortable with my duties as a deputy prosecutor, I began to develop a civil law practice preparing clients' wills, assisting them with selling their homes, and resolving their disputes. As Dirk Montana had mentioned when he told me of the job opening at the Prosecutor's Office, I would be allowed to have a private practice on the side.

Cassandra Whiteman walked into my office for her appointment on Thursday at 2:00 p.m. All I knew about her case was that she had a problem with her show horse and a possible malpractice claim against her veterinarian. Cassie, as she asked me to call her, was an attractive lady, about thirty years of age with a nice friendly smile. With dark brown hair that swept down to her shoulders, she looked a little bit like a rodeo queen in her black and white cowboy boots and tight-fitting jeans.

After exchanging pleasantries, Cassie explained to me that she had taken her two-year-old show horse named Penelope to her vet, Dr. Brahman, for a routine procedure commonly known as a "tail snip." Five days later Penelope's tail fell off.

Probably not the best visual for a show horse, I thought while asking, "What is the purpose of a tail snip procedure?"

"I need to explain that," she said, reaching for her stylish yellow handbag on the floor next to her chair. Cassie then produced a stack of 5" by 7" colored photos as she continued her explanation. "Penelope had the bad habit of swishing her tail during competitions which caused the judges to take valuable points away from her. The more poised and serene the horse during its performance, the higher the marks from the judges. There are tendons on either side at the base of the tail where the tail attaches to the horse's rump. If these tendons are severed, no more tail swishing. The tail will remain fixed throughout the performance," she concluded.

I was busily scribbling notes on my lawyer's trusty yellow legal pad as Cassie continued. "Dr. Brahman performed the procedure Friday afternoon before the Memorial Day weekend but left town right after the surgery, I believe to attend a family reunion at the coast. No one treated the surgical wounds till the following Tuesday when it was too late to save the infected tail," she concluded frowning as she handed me the colored photos. The first half of the stack of photos depicted a beautiful, sleek, dark chestnut mare with a shiny black tail. The remainder of the photos were of the same horse but with no tail.

Cassie then handed me a Bill of Sale establishing she had purchased Penelope a little over a year ago for $30,000. Next, Cassie pushed papers across my desk establishing the horse's superior pedigree.

Even though I was sadly lacking in experience with horses, I was eager to take the case for several reasons. With negligence a virtual given, I concluded that it should be a simple matter of my contacting Dr. Brahman's insurance carrier to get a substantial settlement. A quick negotiated settlement would be a nice payday for me at the standard one-third contingency fee rate. That Cassie appeared to be a most pleasant client was not to be discounted in the equation.

Three weeks had passed since I mailed my brilliant demand letter to Dr. Brahman's insurance carrier, Equine Insurance Ltd. My request for settlement included six large photos of Penelope, three pre and three post tail. I demanded one hundred thousand dollars in damages which I considered a reasonable starting point for negotiation. Two weeks later, having received no response from Equine Insurance, I filed suit in Superior Court asking for damages in the amount of $150,000 thinking that should get their attention. Having no doubt that a jury would love my client, I put in a demand for a 6-person jury trial. But the chances of going to trial with this quirky set of facts seemed remote.

Once the lawsuit was served on Dr. Brahman, I expected that he would confer with Equine Insurance and soon a sizable settlement offer would be forthcoming. We would negotiate a bit, reach an acceptable deal, and in no time, I would be done with this tailless horse case.

Most insurance policies provide that the insurance carrier will pay for an attorney to defend the insured. Since the insurance company is paying for the attorney and for the potential liability of their insured, they have the right to select the attorney of their choice to defend the insured. Equine Insurance hired local attorney Dirk Montana to represent Dr. Brahman. Yes, the same Dirk Montana who was instrumental in my getting my job as a deputy prosecuting attorney. Not a good omen for us, as Dirk had made a career out of successfully defending negligence cases for insurance companies. Dirk had a folksy way about him that made him very effective in front of juries. More importantly, as owner of several race horses, he brought something very significant to the table that I lacked. Horse sense. In summary, Dirk knew a hell of a lot more about horses than I ever would.

In a small town, local lawyers become well acquainted, often developing close friendships outside the courtroom. Would my long-standing relationship with Dirk make it easier to get a good result for Cassie? In fact, just the opposite. Not only do lawyers strive for a good outcome for their clients, but they also are motivated to earn the respect of the opposing attorney. That said, when this case is finally brought to conclusion, Dirk and I will likely play a round of golf together and share a cocktail.

Montana filed his formal Answer to our lawsuit with the court, a standard general denial of any and all liability by the defendant, Dr. Brahman. Thereafter, the Court Clerk set the case for a three-day jury trial to begin on Sept 5th, the Tuesday after the long Labor Day Weekend.

Next followed pretrial discovery which included witnesses' depositions taken under oath to establish what their testimony would be at trial. If the witness fails to be consistent at the time of trial, the deposition can be used to discredit the witness. The deposition process often leads to settlement as both sides have nailed down what the testimony will be at the time of trial and can make better calculations as to the result.

During his deposition, Dr. Brahman confirmed that on May 28th, the Friday before Memorial Day, he had performed the tail snip procedure on Penelope. When I pressed him, he acknowledged he had left town without taking precautions to address the possibility that the surgical wounds could become infected over the long weekend.

My expert witness to confirm Dr. Brahman's negligence was a good friend and golfing buddy, a veterinarian named Dr. Doug McCraney. During his deposition, Dr. McCraney, after reviewing Dr. Brahman's records, confirmed that Dr. Brahman had failed to live up to acceptable medical standards of care by not taking reasonable precautions against infection following the surgery. Most importantly, Dr. McCraney stated that Dr. Brahman's negligence was the proximate cause of the horse losing her tail.

After everyone else had departed my office, Dr. McCraney recounted what he described as his most difficult moment during his deposition. "I was not totally comfortable pointing the finger at Dr. Brahman in case you didn't notice. By the way, I could use a drink. It is 5:00 o'clock," he added.

When I confessed that I had no alcohol in my office, Dr. McCraney responded aggressively. "You call yourself an attorney and you don't keep a bottle of whiskey in your office? What is wrong with you?" He followed his comment with a big grin, but he had made his point. From that day forward, I always kept a bottle of Pendleton Whiskey in the lower right-hand drawer of my desk.

12

In the Best Interest of the Child

The privilege of being a parent is a sacred right under the law. Accordingly, before parental rights can be legally terminated, a very strong case must be presented to a judge (no jury) that it is in the best interest of the child to legally terminate parental rights. Through her actions and inactions, Wanda Fleming, mother of four-year-old Theodore Barton Fleming, had made a compelling case for Judge Bottomly to legally terminate her rights as the parent of little Teddy.

Six months after his birth, The Department of Social and Health Services (DSHS) had removed Teddy from Wanda for abuse/neglect. Neighbors had notified DSHS that Wanda was leaving Teddy home alone in her apartment for lengthy periods of time while he cried continuously. Teddy was placed in foster care with Bill and Norma Robinson while DSHS investigated.

In reviewing the Fleming file, I noted that Judge Bottomly, at various hearings over many months, had required Wanda to attend parenting classes, meet with individuals from Child Protective Services, as well as follow steps outlined by the caseworker, most of which she had ignored. Furthermore, Wanda had failed to attend numerous scheduled visitations with Teddy. Perhaps most dramatically underscoring her failure as a parent was Wanda's lack of contact with Teddy on his birthdays and holidays, including Christmas. Her often repeated excuse for failure to maintain contact with Teddy was her poor health which was contradicted by witnesses who had seen her at local bars. Wanda had also spent considerable time at a drug rehab facility. My notes showed that the father was "unknown."

Meanwhile, as the months turned into years (Teddy had just had his fourth birthday), he was thriving in foster care with Bill and Norma Robinson and their two daughters, ages ten and seven. The notes in my file confirmed that the Robinsons were prepared to adopt Teddy and make him a full-fledged member of their family if the court would allow it.

My job, as deputy prosecuting attorney for the state, was to convince the judge that it was time to terminate Wanda's parental rights so that Teddy could be adopted by the Robinsons. My first witness was the caseworker from DSHS, Margaret Shafer, who, referring to her notes, testified at length of Wanda's many transgressions as a parent. Ms. Shafer detailed by date the meetings Wanda had missed and the scheduled visitations she had ignored. She confirmed that Wanda had made no effort to contact Teddy on his birthdays or on Christmas or other holidays.

Ms. Shafer also testified that Teddy was thriving with his foster family, Bill and Norma Robinson and their two girls. She stated that the Robinsons had expressed a desire to adopt Teddy. My last question to Ms. Shafer was regarding the whereabouts of the father. "Father unknown," she stated matter-of-factly. "We have no indication of any contact from a male during the entire four years of the boy's life."

My next witnesses were Bill and Norma Robinson, both of whom came across as reputable and genuinely concerned with Teddy's wellbeing. Each confirmed independently what Ms. Shafer had just stated. They were desirous of adopting Teddy and making him a full-fledged member of their family if the court would authorize it. Their two girls, Madelyn and Morgan, already considered him their little brother. Both Robinsons testified that there had been virtually no contact from Wanda in the last several months until shortly before today's hearing.

Wanda's court appointed attorney, at state expense, was Reginald Reser. I had been in court up against Reggie on several occasions. At 6'5" and 275 pounds, Reggie had a booming voice that matched his physical presence. The gentle giant always did his best for his clients even though he often was not dealt the best of hands. As the courtroom theater unfolded, I felt a little sorry for Reggie getting stuck with Wanda as his client for the past two and a half years as she was uncooperative and, at times, defiant. At least he was being compensated for his efforts at the standard county rate of $125 per hour for court-appointed attorneys.

After I rested on behalf of the state, Wanda Fleming came forward to testify on her own behalf. Wanda was a large Caucasian woman who, on this day in court, was wearing an oversized pink sweatshirt stamped with *Daytona Beach Racing Team*. With a pale round face and limp dishwater blonde hair, she appeared to be middle aged. Quickly reviewing my file, I confirmed that she was actually only twenty-six years old. From the questions he asked of Wanda, it was apparent that Reggie was attempting to justify her lack of contact with Teddy by having her describe a litany of health problems she had experienced over the past four years. She testified about her mental health challenges and her drug rehab stint. While Wanda's stated health problems might engender sympathy, it struck me that her physical challenges only added weight to the evidence confirming her inability to be an adequate parent, a point I intended to make on closing argument to the judge.

In an effort to establish that Wanda had not totally ignored Teddy's birthdays, Reggie introduced into evidence a recording that Wanda identified as having been made by herself and her friends at McFeeley's Tavern. Once the recording got started, we all suffered through an off-key drunken group rendition of "Happy Birthday to Teddy." The recording might have been hilarious under other circumstances, but, in this situation, it came across as a sad commentary on Wanda's lifestyle and relationship with her son.

It was nearing 5:00 pm as Reser and I both concluded our closing arguments. Taking virtually no time to deliberate, Judge Bottomly ruled from the bench that the state had met its heavy burden of establishing neglect (abandonment) by the parent while holding that it was in the best interest of the child to fully and finally terminate Wanda's parental rights. Upon my request, the judge also terminated the rights of the unknown father, a detail necessary to pave the way for a future adoption by the Robinsons.

Would Wanda appeal Judge Bottomly's decision to terminate her parental rights? From her perspective, she had little to lose. She needed to be able to tell herself and her friends that she had fought the legal system to the very end. And perhaps even more importantly, it wasn't costing her anything. From Reggie's vantage point, he pretty much had to proceed with an appeal or risk a malpractice claim from Wanda down the road.

It was no big surprise when I was served with a formal Notice of Appeal of the Fleming decision to the Washington State Supreme Court. The appellant (Wanda) would submit her brief prepared by Reginald Reser to the Supreme Court. Thereafter, on behalf of the state, as respondent, I would submit my reply brief. Once the briefs were filed, the case would be set on the court docket for a hearing before the nine state Supreme Court justices. We would be traveling across the state to Olympia, capital of the State of

Washington, and the location of the Washington State Supreme Court.

13

Over My Dead Body

Friends were over for dinner. "Excuse me," I apologized to our guests. "I have to pick up a client from the airport and deliver her to her hotel. Should be back in a half an hour or so."

"You can't believe what this is all about," I could hear Claire explaining to our guests as I walked to the kitchen. "He's meeting a rabbi at the airport who is bringing an Orthodox Jewish woman from Seattle. The woman's mother died early this morning in Walla Walla having lived with her son and daughter-in-law the last couple of years. The Jewish daughter is insisting on a Jewish funeral and burial for her mother. The son was raised a Jew and even had a Bar Mitzvah but married a Catholic girl and converted to Catholicism. The son and his wife have lined up a Catholic funeral and burial."

So much for client confidentiality, I thought, grabbing my car keys from the kitchen counter.

"What religion was the mother?" I could hear one of our guests ask just as I shut the kitchen door to the garage behind me.

That's a good question, I thought, backing my Camry out of the driveway for the ten-minute drive to the Walla Walla Municipal Airport.

Through the large glass window facing the tarmac, I watched the dozen or so passengers trudge from the plane toward the little airport terminal. That's got to be the rabbi, I thought, taking in the small but spritely bearded man in a black overcoat two sizes too big for him. Wearing a broad felt hat, the rabbi held a thick dark book in one hand and a battered brown leather brief case in the other. Walking beside the rabbi was a rather plumpish, dark haired middle-aged woman. She had the collar of her forest green overcoat turned up against the evening chill.

As they entered the small terminal, I walked up to them and introduced myself.

"Shalom, young man," the rabbi said pumping my hand. "I am Rabbi Goldfarb. And this is my friend, Carol Levine," he said gesturing to Carol. "As I mentioned on the phone, Carol's mother, Miriam, died only this morning. If we don't do something fast, God forbid, Miriam will be cremated and have a Catholic funeral and burial! Out of this mess, a fine young lawyer like you will bring us some mazel."

"I'm so sorry to be causing you all this trouble," Carol offered apologetically while giving me a brave smile. Her face was drawn and her eyes red. To be expected with the loss of her mother, I thought.

"My condolences for your loss," I said to Carol, gently patting her elbow.

"Listen," the rabbi said from the back seat of the Camry as we exited the airport parking lot. "We will go to the funeral home, grab Miriam, and take her to Seattle on the early morning flight, and our tsuris is over!" he declared triumphantly.

I swallowed and responded, "That's just totally impossible," my voice cracking ever so slightly. "In the first place, body snatching is a crime. Secondly, I still plan to practice law after you leave town." Having been an attorney for just over a year, I was uncomfortable with the direction the rabbi was steering us.

"What religion was your mother?" I asked Carol as we entered her room at the Travelodge, "It seems that should help decide this dispute."

"That's where the problem arises," she responded. "You see, my mother was a devout Jew for the first 86 years of her life. My father, God rest his soul, was a devout Jew as well. Dad is buried in Beit Shalom Cemetery north of Seattle. There is a pre-purchased plot right next to dad just waiting for mom. My parents raised both their children in the Jewish faith. Norman had a Bar Mitzvah and I had a Bat Mitzvah in the family synagogue. Norman's wife, Julia, is a devout Catholic. To accommodate Julia, Norman converted to Catholicism about ten years ago. At first it really bothered mom but she began to accept it as something she couldn't change."

"After mom started getting forgetful about two years ago, she moved in with Norm and Julia. With the change of scenery, her dementia got progressively worse. Norman says that mom had been going to Mass with them every week for the last year and that they plan to have her cremated followed by a Catholic funeral. I personally don't think she knew which end was up the last year or so," Carol concluded as the tears began to flow down her flushed cheeks.

“Not to worry,” the rabbi said reassuring Carol. “We have this brilliant young attorney on our side now. Everything will work out.”

“I’ve got to get back to dinner now. I left my wife hanging with our guests. You two meet me in my office tomorrow morning at 8:30 a.m. It’s just eight blocks west on Main Street,” I said pointing down town. “129 West Main Street. I will call Norman tonight and see if I can get him there to meet with us. Let’s see if there is any possibility that we can resolve this dispute without the need to go to court to get an Injunction. An agreed resolution will be far less stressful for all, and far less expensive,” I added. “Furthermore there is no guarantee what a judge would do with this situation.”

“Thanks so much for coming out tonight. We will see you at your office tomorrow,” Carol said squeezing my arm and giving me a smile. She seemed much more relaxed now that she was settling into her room.

The rabbi was following me out to my car. “Listen,” he said, his eyes lighting up. “There is nothing to keep us from going to the funeral home right now. We will grab the body and save everybody time, trouble, and money.”

Here we go again, I thought. "Rabbi, I told you we are not going to go body snatching tonight or any other night. We're going to be completely legal and above board or you are going to have to do it without me," I concluded emphatically.

Standing by my car, Rabbi Goldfarb raised his palms up toward the darkened sky, paused for a brief moment as if expecting to get direction from above. Suddenly dropping his hands to his side, he then responded, "Okay, I suppose we have to do it your way. I have every confidence that you can resolve this for us. So go home already young man. Get a good night's sleep. You are going to need to be sharp in the morning," he winked.

Driving home from the airport, I asked aloud to the empty passenger seat, "How do I manage to get myself into the middle of these bizarre situations?"

"You got back sooner than I expected," Claire said as I entered our kitchen from the garage. "You made it back just in time for dessert."

"Just need to make one more phone call and I'll be with you," I promised.

Punching in the phone number Carol had provided, I wondered how I was going to open the conversation with Norman.

"Hello," Norman answered. "Yes, this is Norm Shankland."

I introduced myself and expressed my condolences regarding the passing of his mother. Next, I explained that his sister, Carol, had flown in this evening from Seattle with her rabbi. I explained that Carol had hired me to represent her. When I emphasized how important it was to Carol that their mother have a Jewish funeral and burial, I waited for his response, but there was silence at the other end. After a long pause, I asked Norman if he would be willing to meet with us in my law office at 9:00 a.m. tomorrow morning to discuss the matter with the goal of hopefully resolving the dispute amicably rather than going to court. I was making certain that if he did not acquiesce, Norman understood Carol was prepared to start court proceedings.

Another pause, and then Norman replied, "I'll come to your law office tomorrow morning to talk to my sister. Will try to be there about 9:00 a.m." Then he hung up without another word.

Making a quick calculus of Norman's motivations, it struck me that he was caught in the middle of this religious quarrel between his wife and his sister. Unfortunately, from my client's standpoint, Norman's decision would be based upon the fact that he would have to live every day with his wife while his sister would ultimately be far across the state in Seattle. Despite these family dynamics, I took it as a positive that Norm was at least willing to meet with us tomorrow morning.

As I brushed my teeth before bed, Claire asked, "I wonder why it matters so much that their mother have a Jewish funeral?"

Spitting a mouth full of tooth paste and water into the sink, I replied, "Fair question. I am going to find that out first thing in the morning. That is unless the rabbi carries out his plan tonight against my advice," I added.

"What plan is that?" she asked turning out the bedroom light.

"The rabbi wants to snatch the body from Herring Funeral Home and leave town with Miriam before anyone is the wiser. I did my best to dissuade him. He is a real piece of work," I added.

At 8:30 a.m. the next morning, I ushered Rabbi Goldfarb and Carol Levine into my office. The rabbi was dressed in the same outfit he had worn yesterday evening. From the quizzical looks on the secretaries' faces, it was obvious they had not been around many orthodox rabbis in our isolated farming community.

Now both Carol and the rabbi were seated in my office across from me in the high-backed tan leather chairs I had just acquired from the wife of an elderly attorney who had recently died.

"Good news," I began. "Norman has agreed to meet with us this morning. He promised he will be here at 9:00 a.m. Before he arrives, it would be helpful, Rabbi, if you would explain the importance of Miriam having a Jewish funeral and burial."

Contemplating my request, the rabbi took off his broad brimmed felt hat and stroked his wispy beard while repositioning himself in his chair. Sensing the rabbi was about to embark on a lengthy discussion, I reached for my cup of coffee.

"You see young man," the rabbi began, "The first rule among Orthodox Jews is that there must be no cremation of the body. This is based on the old Orthodox belief in resurrection of the soul which will be reunited with the body. For this reason, cremation is not possible. This belief originated at least 600 years before Christ when the Jews were held in captivity by the Babylonians. Our idea of resurrection has been in existence long before the Christians came up with it," he pointed out proudly.

"Before you continue," I interrupted, "Would you care for a cup of coffee?" I asked.

"I do not drink coffee," the rabbi responded. "But do you know where I might be able to find a kosher lunch in this town? I haven't eaten since yesterday morning."

"My apologies, but I don't think we have a kosher restaurant," I responded feeling sorry for the rabbi.

He continued. "In addition to there being no cremation, Orthodox Jews believe there should not be an embalming of the body nor should there be any attempt to make the deceased look lifelike. A small group from the congregation called the Chevra Kadisha prepares the body for burial. The cadaver is thoroughly cleansed and wrapped in a white shroud. The deceased will lay in the shroud overnight before the burial. All night long, two people, part of the Chevra Kadisha, will attend the body while chanting prayers. The attendants are often furnished with a fifth of whiskey," he winked at me, "to help them get through the long night."

"Following the funeral, the close relatives sit on low cushions for a period of one week. Prayers are recited three times a day. All mirrors are covered to emphasize the vanity of daily life. To demonstrate the intensity of the family's grief, male family members will commonly cut a piece of lapel right out of their suits, thus ruining the suit for future use. In today's world, sometimes a piece of fabric from another garment is pinned to the lapel as a symbolic gesture. Suits have gotten so expensive! I should emphasize that these rituals I have described are followed by only the most orthodox of Jews."

"Rabbi," I interrupted. "I just watched a television documentary which told the story of the ancient hill top rock fortress in Israel called Masada. The vastly outnumbered Jews defending the high ground heroically held off the large Roman army for many weeks. When defeat became inevitable, the Jews committed mass suicide rather than become slaves of the Romans in defeat. I'm curious. How does the Jewish religion view the act of suicide?"

Licking his chops at the prospect of answering my question, the rabbi started in once again. "The word

Masada means fortress in Hebrew. Most Jewish holidays commemorate a great military victory or freedom from the bonds of slavery. What could be a greater moment in Jewish history than that of the outnumbered Jews of Masada, against all odds, holding off the mighty Roman army? So why is there no Jewish holiday to celebrate this memorable event? As you mentioned, the siege ended with a group suicide by the Jewish zealots as the only alternative to being conquered. Suicide is a taboo within the Jewish religion. Hence, no holiday commemorating the heroics of the Jews at Masada and really no acknowledgement whatsoever of these events until about 70 years ago. Now tour buses deposit hundreds of tourists at Masada every day of the week except Saturday so that tourists can see up close where the Masada heroics actually occurred. It seems the tourist dollars far outweigh the suicide taboo," he concluded with a wry smile.

We were interrupted by the intercom buzzing on my desk. "There is a Norman Shankland here to see you," the voice on the intercom announced.

"Send him in," I replied to the box.

In his mid-sixties, Norman had black and gray curly hair and a friendly smile. He was wearing a navy-blue sweater, stretched a bit over his sizeable paunch, khaki slacks and dark blue Nike tennis shoes. Norm and his sister embraced warmly, sharing their grief at the recent loss of their mother. As they separated, Carol wiped her eyes while Norman blew his nose into his handkerchief. The rabbi and I exchanged a look that said we both had failed to anticipate this emotional moment shared by brother and sister following the recent death of their mother.

"Look," Norm began as he put his handkerchief back into his pocket. "I realize it's important to you, Carol, but the arrangements have all been made. Julia and I have decided mom will receive a Catholic funeral and burial. She wanted to be cremated."

The rabbi jumped in. "The lady was born a Jew and was a Jew her whole life! Let her be buried as one!" he argued forcefully.

"Rabbi, let's leave the two of them alone to talk," I quickly interceded. To my surprise, without objection, the rabbi followed me out of my office. As we departed, I overheard a bit of the conversation between Carol and Norman.

"Does it really matter to you one way or the other?" Carol questioned her brother.

"I guess I never expected all these problems," Norman said dropping his head into his hands and heaving a sigh.

The rabbi and I walked across the hall to the coffee room. I did not offer him coffee.

"I'll just take water," he said. "But seriously, is there any place I can find kosher food in this town?"

"I'm afraid I can't help you there," I said chuckling as I poured myself a steaming cup of black coffee. "But I can offer you an apple from our mini fridge."

Fifteen minutes later the rabbi and I reentered my office. The tension level had dropped noticeably. Both Carol and Norman were smiling.

"It's settled!" Carol said excitedly. "And Norman says he'll pay for half the cost to have mom flown back with me to Seattle!" she announced while giving Norman another hug.

"Mazel tov!" the rabbi exclaimed. Without missing a beat, he then turned to me and directed, "You will make the arrangements with the funeral home to deliver Miriam to the airport. We can still make the afternoon flight," he exclaimed, his eyes shining through his rimless glasses.

"Julia is not going to be happy with the turn of events, but I'll deal with her," Norman said matter-of-factly. He then quietly shut my office door behind him.

"Mazel tov!" the rabbi repeated excitedly as he pumped my hand. "A job well done!"

"How can I ever thank you enough!" Carol said with tears in her eyes as she embraced me.

"Thank him when he gives you his bill," the rabbi quipped.

"Getting you and Norm together to work it out was all it took," I responded. "But I'm curious. What changed Norman's mind?"

"I'm convinced he just never fully realized how important our family's Jewish traditions are to me until we were able to speak face to face. I think telling him what our dad would have wanted was the tipping point. And I have my doubts he really cared that much one way or the other. I think he was just trying to please Julia. Now that he's caved in to me, I hope she's not too hard on him."

As they stood waiting for the elevator, I could hear the rabbi's voice. "Now let's see if we can find some kosher food around this village before the afternoon flight. With what this young man will charge us, we better eat while we have the chance!"

"What was all that about?" my secretary asked as she placed the morning mail on the corner of my desk.

"Just a little holy war between the Romans and the Jews," I explained.

"Who shall we say won?" she asked.

"I suppose you could say the Jews won the battle," I responded. "But they paid a heavy price for victory."

"How's that?"

"They almost starved to death," I replied as I googled the phone number for Herring Funeral Home where Miriam was resting peacefully, oblivious to the tug of war over her dead body.

14
Sleeping With the Enemy

My carry-on suitcase was packed and I was on my way to the Washington State Supreme Court in Olympia. I would be appearing on behalf of the state with the goal of upholding the decision of the trial court on the case of In re The Welfare of Theordore Barton Fleming. If I were successful, four-year-old Teddy Fleming would thereafter be adopted by his welcoming and capable foster family, the Robinsons, where he had resided for the past three years.

To get to Olympia I would fly commercially from Walla Walla to Seattle, land at SeaTac, rent a car, and drive an hour on I-5 south to Olympia. Prior to my flight I checked in at the little Walla Walla Municipal

Airport terminal, but was advised by the ticket agent that the Alaska Airlines flight to SeaTac would be at least forty minutes late. It was then I saw Reggie waving at me from the doorway of THE BLUE YONDER, the small airport bar across the lobby.

"Let me buy you a drink," he offered. "Looks like the flight is delayed at least forty minutes." I quickly ducked into the dimly lit bar for a cocktail before the flight departed. After I had downed my drink, I circled back to the ticket counter to check on the flight only to learn that it was further delayed. Now back in the bar, I offered to buy a second round.

Reggie explained that Wanda, Teddy's biological mother, would not be coming to Olympia for the hearing. "Health issues again," he shrugged. "Hey, why don't we share a rental car for the drive from SeaTac to Olympia?" Reggie suggested. "Save Walla Walla County a little money."

"Sounds like a plan to me," I replied thinking it would be nice to have a traveling companion for the two-day trip even if he were the attorney arguing against me in court. We were just finishing our second drink when the airline agent stuck his head in the bar announcing that the plane was getting ready to taxi down the runway. We grabbed our briefcases, each threw some cash on our table, and raced out to the plane. We managed to scramble aboard just prior to the door closing behind us.

Upon arrival at SeaTac, Reggie trotted off to baggage claim to retrieve his checked suitcase while I rolled my carry-on suitcase to the rental car area. When Reggie met me at our silver Chevy Malibu rental car, he was holding only his brief case in hand. No suitcase. "I called Walla Walla," he blurted out, visibly agitated. "They never loaded my damn suitcase on the plane. It's still in Walla Walla. Soonest they can get it here is noon tomorrow. Lot of good that will do me with a 9:00 a.m. hearing in front of the f*cking Supremes tomorrow!"

For the first time, I scrutinized Reggie's attire, as it was now obvious that he would have no opportunity to upgrade his wardrobe before our hearing in the morning. Trying hard to avoid a case of schadenfreude (after all, he was opposing counsel), I took in the details. Blue and white gingham cowboy style shirt, complete with pearl pocket snaps, khaki pants, brown penny loafers and a brown leather bomber jacket. I guess it could be worse. At least he wasn't wearing jeans, I thought, as I placed my suitcase in the trunk of the Malibu.

"Not looking good for me at the moment," a distraught Reggie lamented as he folded his large frame into the passenger seat. "Maybe having a steak dinner at my favorite restaurant at County expense will brighten my mood," he announced as he fastened his seat belt. Disregarding my triskaidekaphobia, I drove the five minutes from the airport to the nearby 13 Coins Restaurant where we were quickly seated. The service was slow and it was getting late before our large T-bone steaks finally arrived. It was after 9:00 p.m. before we were back in our silver Malibu driving south on I-5 through a Puget Sound downpour.

It was still raining hard when we finally arrived in the parking lot of The Fairfield Inn and Suites, Reggie's hotel. I told Reggie I would wait in the car to make sure that he still had a room before I drove to the Marriott. Five minutes later, he was back, standing by my car window, his shoulders slumped, the rain dripping off his soaked dark hair.

"My sorry evening continues," he announced looking down at me. "They sold my room. Can you believe it? The state legislature starts tomorrow so the town is crawling with people looking for hotel rooms. I had them call around to see if there were any vacancies. They are telling me that every room in town is booked," he shrugged.

"Jump in," I said. "Let's go to the Marriot and see what they can do for you at my hotel. Hope they are still holding my room for me or we will both be spending the night in this car."

To my great relief, the pleasant male desk clerk at the Marriott confirmed that I still had my guaranteed room. He also reiterated that every room in town had been rented because of the aforementioned commencement of the legislative session. While a disaster for Reggie, the legislature was obviously a boon to the local hotel industry. Translation. No room for Reggie anywhere in Olympia.

I couldn't just leave the big guy out on the street. Or could I? Afterall, he was the opposition in court tomorrow. Should I at least offer him the car for the night? Upon inquiry, the desk clerk confirmed that they had one rollaway bed remaining in storage which could be delivered to my room for an additional $20. Without further thought, I put the rollaway bed on my room charges while the desk clerk handed Reggie a survival pack full of toiletries.

"Well Reggie," I announced as we walked down the carpeted hallway searching for Room 213. "It appears that opposing counsel will be bunking together the night before we appear in front of the Supremes."

"Let's agree to keep the hotel arrangements to ourselves if you don't mind," Reggie muttered as I opened the door to our room. "And by the way, I owe you big time for this," he added.

"It will be our own personal N.D.A., (Non-Disclosure Agreement)," I replied.

"Deal," he nodded.

Soon there was a knock on our door. The rollaway bed was delivered and set up near the window. "Sorry about the small bed, but this is our last rollaway," the helpful bellhop announced as Reggie slipped him a couple of dollars.

The child-sized bed was narrow and no more than six feet long. Just as I was wondering how Reggie was going to fit into that bed, he interrupted my thoughts. "Check this out!" he exclaimed in his booming voice. On the bedside table was a large glass bowl filled with ice. Stashed randomly in the ice were six bottles of Olympia beer. Next to the bowl was a message typed on a white sheet of paper that read: "The Courtyard by Marriot welcomes you to the opening of the

Washington State Legislative Session. Please have an Olympia beer on us and enjoy your stay!"

"When in Olympia, drink Olympia beer," Reggie chortled as he popped a cold one and handed a dripping, ice-cold bottle to me. Twenty minutes later, when I reached for a second beer, I realized Reggie had already polished off the remaining four. Now sprawled across the queen-sized bed and still fully clothed except for having removed his shoes, Reggie was snoring away contentedly.

My miniature rollaway bed was lumpy and too soft. Reggie never quit snoring the whole night. At some point I must have fallen asleep, but when my alarm woke me at 7:00 a.m., my shoulders were stiff and my back ached. Limping to the bathroom in the dimly lit hotel room, I noted that the queen-sized bed was empty. Reggie was long gone. I recalled that before he conked out last night, he mentioned something about going over early to the law library adjacent to the courthouse to fine tune his argument.

While brushing my teeth, I began to wonder how Reggie got over to the courthouse? Had he taken the rental car and left me stranded? Racing to the window, I was relieved to see that the silver Malibu was still parked in the lot two floors below. The black key fob was sitting on the dresser. After a hot shower, I put on my attorney's uniform for the court hearing, a white dress shirt, navy blue and silver striped tie, and charcoal gray three-piece suit. My laced shiny black leather shoes completed the look. A quick complimentary breakfast in the hotel lounge, and I was off to the State Supreme Court.

Gazing around the beautiful high-ceilinged cathedral-like Temple of Justice, I noted that there were at least a dozen attorneys, all formally dressed in suits, milling about, waiting their turns for the bailiff to call their respective cases. That is, with the exception of Reggie, who was dressed exactly as he was last night except for a few more wrinkles in his cowboy shirt.

We were third on the court docket. I half listened to the arguments of the attorneys involved in the two cases preceding ours. When the bailiff announced, "In re The Welfare of Theodore Barton Fleming," I walked ahead of Reggie down the aisle passing a dozen evenly spaced spectator benches as I made my way to the counsel table. Looming a good eight feet above us sat the nine black-robed intimidating justices. I had been forewarned that it was common practice for the justices to interrupt the attorneys' oral arguments to ask questions. Typically, the justice asking the questions was the one assigned to review the briefs and trial transcript in our case, which made sense since that particular justice would have the best grasp of the facts and law. Presumably the justice assigned to our case would also have great sway with the others in coming up with a final decision. It would be interesting to learn which justice I needed to win over.

I took a few deep breaths. Surveying the black-robed justices all seated in a row above me, it struck me that they closely resembled a line of crows sitting on a telephone wire, a visual that caused me to relax a bit.

As the appellant (the one appealing the trial court's decision), Reginald Reser would go first. Since the justices had been provided with a copy of the Fleming trial transcript as well as our briefs, presumably they already had a good grasp of the case background.

As Reggie approached the podium in his casual attire to begin his argument, there were some quizzical looks from the justices. "I want to apologize for my appearance this morning, Your Honors," Reggie began in his deep booming voice. "Last night my suitcase was lost by the airline somewhere between Walla Walla and SeaTac leaving me stuck with the clothing I wore on the plane." There followed sympathetic chuckles from the justices, all of whom undoubtably could relate to airline baggage problems.

A smart move by Reggie, I thought. By commencing with the apology and the missing luggage explanation, he had inserted a human element into his presentation that effectively transformed his inappropriate attire into a positive. After Reggie's unique introduction, the case pretty much proceeded according to script. Reggie attempted to justify Wanda's lack of contact with her son by emphasizing her significant health problems. After repeating most of Wanda's health issues to the justices, he concluded by arguing that with proper counseling and parental training, Wanda could be a great mother.

It was now my turn as the respondent representing the prevailing party at the trial court level, namely the State of Washington. My butterflies quickly dissipated as I listed the many chances the lower court had provided Wanda to regain custody. I detailed her failure to maintain the most basic of contact with Teddy, missing his birthdays and holidays. I listed her failure to utilize social services provided to her to improve her parenting skills. Just as I was on a roll emphasizing that the state had jumped through all the requisite legal hoops to meet its heavy burden of terminating parental rights, old Justice Filmore Pike, seated above me on the far right, interrupted me.

"Counsel," Justice Pike barked. "Is it fair to terminate this mother's parental rights if she has had all these health problems?"

My initial reaction to the justice's interruption was pure panic. My mind began racing to construct a persuasive answer.

"I'm glad you asked that question, Your Honor." I began, buying time to gather my thoughts. Fortunately, I had anticipated that a question of this type might be asked. "I will answer your question on two levels, Justice Pike. First, the mother's medical problems were not substantiated by either her medical providers or her witnesses. In fact, the record will reflect that Wanda was spending a good amount of her free time socializing in bars. Secondly, even if her medical issues were verified, the fact remains that this mother abandoned her child in every sense of the word. She ignored his birthdays, Christmas and other holidays. In fact, she seldom visited him or checked up on him over a three-year period of time. And finally, assuming for the moment that the mother truly has substantial health issues, it nevertheless remains in the best interest of the child to terminate the mother's parental rights. Furthermore, the record will show that, over the past three plus years the child has been fully integrated into the foster parents' family. The foster parents testified in court that they are prepared to adopt the child if parental rights are terminated."

"Thank you," Justice Pike said while quickly nodding his head in my direction, a gesture I took to signal his approval of my response.

I concluded my remarks by emphasizing that terminating Wanda's parental rights was Teddy's best hope for a normal, happy childhood, ultimately leading to his becoming a productive and contributing member of society.

The chief justice thanked us for our presentations while stating that we could expect a written decision in a few weeks. He then added, "Off the record, Mr. Reser, I appreciate your acknowledging that you were not properly dressed for your appearance in front of the court today. During my last trip to a judicial conference in New York, the airline lost my suitcase for a full week! You have our sympathies." More chuckles from the justices.

As we walked up the aisle to the back of the court room, the bailiff announced the next case. For the first time, I realized that my shirt was soaked through from perspiration, both back and front. The good news was that I had survived my first appearance in front of the Supremes and given it my best for Teddy. All things considered, I had a good feeling that the Court would make the right decision.

When our plane landed in Walla Walla that evening, Reggie's suitcase was waiting for him at the ticket counter. Unable to resist, I remarked, "Hey Reggie, if you want to take a trip somewhere, you are already fully packed." Still wearing his cowboy shirt, Reggie either didn't hear me or he chose to ignore me. It had been a long two days for him.

15

Whoa is Me

Turning the calendar from August to September, I noted that the trial date for my tailless horse case was fast approaching. With less than a week before trial, there still had been no hint of a settlement offer. On the wild chance that the case would actually go to trial, I began educating myself about show horses. Somewhere during the course of my reading, I learned that the tail snipping procedure has been deemed unethical, and, in many states, flatly illegal, a detail Attorney Montana was certain to make known to the jury. This bit of new information made my stomach churn as my vision of a fat settlement had all but evaporated.

Cassie was seated across from me at my desk. It was Friday morning before the trial which was set to begin after the Labor Day weekend. Cassie held a hairy rope-like object in her hands. "I thought you would need the tail to present to the jury at the trial," Cassie explained handing me the thick black tail.

Until the moment that the tail was splayed across my desk, it had not occurred to me that very soon I would be in front of a jury presenting the severed tail in evidence as plaintiff's Exhibit Number One. I explained to Cassie that I had learned that the tail snipping procedure was an illegal practice in many states, while considered unethical pretty much everywhere else. From her reaction, I gathered she already had an awareness of this information. "I'm leaving it in your capable hands," she said, giving me a reassuring smile as she departed my office.

Now alone and pondering the black horse tail on my desk, I visualized myself parading in front of the men and women jurors as the trial began. Waving the horse's tail under the jurors' noses, I announced, "Ladies and gentlemen of the jury. You are about to hear a tale of whoa!"

Awakening from my reverie, I called Montana's office to inquire as to whether there might be the slightest possibility of a last-minute settlement. I was not yet ready to grovel, but I was getting close. Montana's secretary, Diana, advised me that Dirk was out at the fairgrounds at the racetrack. He had left word that if I wanted to talk settlement, I should come out to the horse barns adjacent to the track. The mere mention of a settlement was music to my ears. The thought of bringing a lawsuit before a jury on behalf of a tailless horse was beginning to feel more than a bit embarrassing. Additionally, I knew that I was no match for Dirk Montana when it came to equine expertise. If only I could find a graceful way out, I would vow never to touch another horse case the rest of my life, tailless or otherwise.

As I turned into the gravel parking lot next to the fairgrounds on that warm sunny afternoon, The Walla Walla Fair and Frontier Days was going full bore. From the lot, one could see the ferris wheel rotating and hear the joyous screams of kids as the roller-coaster rose and fell. Before making my way to the admission gate, I deposited my neck tie in the back seat of my car and rolled up my shirt sleeves. I paid the $8.00 admission fee at the ticket window and wandered through the carnival area, dodging excited kids as I proceeded toward the grandstands. The sweet smell of caramel corn drifted over me.

I passed several horse stalls before spotting Dirk Montana perched on a hay bale. He was sipping a beer from a silver can, his ample belly protruding over his silver belt buckle. In faded blue jeans and blue and white western shirt, Dirk greeted me in his low baritone, "Good to see ya. Have a seat." With a wide grin showing the split in his front teeth, Dirk handed me a Coors Light and I plopped down next to him on the hay bale. "Let's see if we can work something out," he opened. "I talked with my client before I left the office this morning. Equine Insurance Company has given me authority to settle the claim for $15,000."

At last we finally had an offer, even though I knew the figure was too low given that Cassie had paid $30,000 for the horse.

Having made the offer, Dirk began posturing. "That's as high as they are willing to go. You've got problems with the legality of that procedure. I strongly suggest you take the offer and consider it a victory with all the issues you've got, that tail snip thing being illegal and all," he concluded.

Because we had not yet received an offer, Cassie and I hadn't discussed an acceptable settlement figure, but I knew it would take more than half of what she had paid for the horse.

"That's totally unreasonable," I replied. "And you are the one with the problems. Your client was clearly negligent or the tail would not have fallen off. That severed tail is our Exhibit #1. The horse cost her $30,000 plus all the training expenses and vet bills. You've gotta do better than $15,000 or we are going to trial." I countered, sounding much more confident than I felt.

"Let me give my client a call and see if they are willing to move up a bit to get this done," he replied, taking a sip of his beer. Digging into the pocket of his jeans for his cell phone, Dirk went outside to make his call in private. Left alone in the sweltering horse barn, I mopped the sweat that was dripping off my forehead. The warm aroma of the stables drifted over me as I sat there, sipping my beer, hoping against hope that Dirk would get the authority to up the ante to a level that would be satisfactory to Cassie. I needed out of this mess.

Dirk was back. He started in again. "I'm not going to bullshit you or dink ya around. My client will pay $30,000 and that's it. Otherwise, we go to trial," he concluded emphatically, and I believed him.

"I'll see if we can make that work," I replied, pushing myself up from the hay bale to call Cassie with the offer which I felt was fair, all things considered. Who knew what a jury would do with this case?

Now outside in the shade of the horse barn, I pulled out my cell phone and conveyed the offer to Cassie. I explained that the initial offer was for $15,000 which I had declined knowing she would want more than half of what she paid for the horse. I told her that we had been negotiating back and forth and now had an offer on the table of $30,000 which I believed to be the best we could do short of going to trial.

"I think this is a reasonable offer," I explained. We have no idea what a jury will do, given that the procedure was borderline illegal. My advice to you is to take the offer and consider it a victory." Pausing, I added, "And I'll lower my contingent fee to twenty-five percent since we are completing the settlement short of a trial." I was hoping that this additional sweetener would be the clincher for her. I held my breath.

"I really appreciate all you have done," Cassie began. "And I never wanted to go to trial. I think their offer is fair and will be very pleased with the result, but I want one addition." There was a long pause. In a voice that cracked with emotion, she said, "I want to keep Penelope!"

"O.K. I'll see if I can finalize it on that basis," I quickly replied. I couldn't imagine why the insurance company would want to acquire the horse but maybe I was missing something. My limited knowledge of horses did not extend to whether or not a tailless horse had any monetary value. Breeding, perhaps?

Back in the horse barn, I announced, "Dirk, my client will agree to accept your offer on condition that she can keep the horse."

"I'll make that work. We have a deal," he said shaking my hand. Then he reached his fist deep into his Igloo cooler and pulled out two more icy cold beers.

"Oh, and by the way. She wants to keep the tail as well," I couldn't resist adding. Dirk let out a loud belly laugh as we clinked our silver beer cans together, toasting our settlement.

16

She's Loaded!

My first client today was Beatrice Elkins, an 88-year-old widow who had three children and six grandchildren. Her name sounded vaguely familiar but I couldn't quite place where I had known her. Mrs. Elkins had made an appointment to update her will. Before inviting her into my office, I quickly reviewed my will questionnaire form filled out by each client interested in having me prepare a new will for them. When completed, this form helped me target unique issues such as the need for estate tax planning or addressing the issue of a child with special needs. A side benefit to the completed form was that it helped my secretary correctly spell all the names set forth in the will.

A quick summary of the most pertinent information provided by Mrs. Elkins was as follows:

Name: Beatrice Alice Elkins

Age: 88

Marital Status: Widow

Spouse: Harold Vance Elkins (Deceased)

List full names of all Children: 3 kids all with Harold, two girls, Alice Marie Martin, age 59, Anita Spencer, age 57 and one boy, William Charles Elkins, age 54; no deceased children

List the extent of your assets (this information will be kept strictly confidential): I will discuss my assets at our meeting.

Set forth any unique circumstances such as estranged children or children with special needs or other: All 3 children have different financial situations. Alice is going thru a divorce. Will discuss further at our meeting.

Beatrice and her friend, a woman of similar age, were seated across from me at my conference table. Beatrice began, "Please call me Bea. I knew your dad when I was a nurse at the V.A. Hospital. I worked on Ward Two with him for thirty years," she continued in her raspy smoker's voice that made me want to offer her a throat lozenge. "Your dad was my favorite doctor in the entire hospital. Never saw him in a hurry. Always calm and had time for everyone. A smart man." Beatrice continued, "I want to introduce my good friend and neighbor, Phyllis Boros. I brought Phyllis along for moral support."

Phyllis raised her wrinkled right-hand shoulder high, and in a throaty voice that red flagged "smoker" as well, stated, "I promise to keep quiet."

"That would be a first," Beatrice chortled and then lapsed into an extended hacking cough.

I took in Bea's purple polyester pants and matching purple blouse. A closer examination of her rosy cheeks revealed it was just makeup applied too liberally. The untamed bun of red hair above her wrinkled face looked like it had been perched on the top of her head by a couple of nesting birds. Her friend, Phyllis, sporting short bleached blond hair, was decked out in a stretchy black pantsuit and a hot pink scarf.

Completing the pleasantries, I began the nuts and bolts of my questioning concerning information I would need to complete Beatrice's will. "How would you like to distribute your estate when you pass?" I asked Beatrice. As always, I intentionally avoided the use of the words "death" and "die" in the conversation but instead used euphemisms such as "when you pass" or "when you are no longer with us."

“I am just torn on that very question,” Bea began theatrically and then described her dilemma regarding her future bequests to her children. “My son, Billy, is a wealthy real estate developer. Bill has more money than God. He and his wife travel the world. Alice is a schoolteacher. Anita is disabled and lives on her Social Security check, month to month. Both girls could really use the money.”

“In my experience,” I responded, “even though the kids have different financial situations, if you treat them unequally, you can easily create bad feelings among the three kids. Then glancing at my will Questionnaire form, I noted, “You don’t seem to have completed your list of assets for me to review. That information is critical for me to properly advise you. Can you give me an idea of how much you have in bank accounts and investment accounts? Do you own your own home? Let’s start with your bank accounts,” I suggested, waiting with blue pen poised over my lined yellow legal pad.

With a sideways glance at Phyllis who was all ears, Beatrice replied hesitantly, “I’m not prepared to provide that information today.” It was obvious Beatrice was not comfortable disclosing her financial status in the presence of her nosey neighbor. Just why Beatrice brought Phyllis along to this private meeting was a mystery to me. Maybe it had something to do with her trepidation regarding meeting with a lawyer.

"Did I mention I have six grandchildren and two great-grandchildren, and the great-grandchildren live in Walla Walla?" announced Beatrice with pride.

"Two great-grandchildren living right here? That is awesome! How old are they?" I asked.

"Luca is three-and-a-half and Jaden will be two soon. They are the sweetest little guys," she swooned. "I just love having them so close by."

Smiling at her enthusiasm, I continued. "When you come back for your next appointment, bring with you a list of all of your assets and debts so I can do a better job advising you." Implicit in my suggestion was that Bea should come alone next time so that she could talk freely. "We can, however, talk today about other important issues such as who you want to be the executor of your will if something should happen to you. We can also discuss who you wish to act on your behalf under a power of attorney for business and healthcare if you should become disabled or incompetent prior to your passing. By law, the power of attorney terminates on your demise when the executor named in your will takes over to resolve your estate."

"I'll give some thought to naming my executor and discuss it with you when I come back for my next appointment," Beatrice said, clutching her bright red purse and standing up abruptly. Together the two elderly ladies shuffled out of my office moving very slowly down the hall. I last saw them entering the restroom together as I closed my office door.

Returning to my desk, I checked my email. An old client was requesting an updated power of attorney. Next email. Would I be interested in a referral on a contract dispute? Next email. Confirmed golf tee time for Saturday at 1:07 p.m. My usual foursome. I was daydreaming about debuting my new Scotty Cameron putter on Saturday when my reverie was broken by a rap, rap, rap on my heavy oak door. It was Bea's friend, Phyllis Boros. There was no sign of Bea whom I assumed was still busy in the bathroom. Phyllis stuck her peroxide head in through the semi open door, and, cupping her right hand around the side of her mouth, she leaned toward me. In a gravelly stage whisper, she advised, "She's loaded!" Then Phyllis quickly turned around, shut the door, and was gone.

17

The Disneyland Dad

Although I found the emotional aspects of practicing family law (divorces) unsettling, it did pay the bills. Washington became a no-fault divorce state way back in 1973. This means that, theoretically, a marriage can be terminated without proof of wrongdoing by either party, such as adultery or cruelty. By merely alleging in the initial Petition for Dissolution of Marriage that the marriage is irretrievably broken, and waiting the specified ninety days, a divorce can be finalized. That said, bad behavior still remains relevant when dealing with child custody, visitation, and even property disputes. More recently, Washington divorce procedures strongly encourage mediation before a divorce case can proceed to trial in front of a judge. Effective mediators, usually attorneys trained in mediation skills, often facilitate settlement, thereby avoiding the need to go to trial.

Vanessa Vivalde swept into my office on a crisp fall morning dressed in a belted cashmere coat and a black and red Hermes scarf around her neck. An attractive blond in her mid-thirties, she placed her well-worn divorce papers in front of me.

"I hear you're pretty good," Vanessa began. "I'd like your opinion on whether I can get sole custody of my daughter. My ex has been a real jerk ever since I filed."

Picking up the coffee-stained divorce decree, I replied, "Give me a little background."

"Mediation was a total failure," Vanessa began. "After a two-day trial before the judge, Matt and I were awarded joint custody of our daughter, Amanda, who is now ten years old. I need to gain full custody of Mandy so I can get some control of the situation. Her father is the all-time Disneyland Dad. When he has Mandy, he lets her ignore her homework, constantly showers her with gifts, and tells her there are no rules when she's in his house. At the end of her visits with Disney Dad, Mandy is totally unmanageable for days."

Leaning back in my chair, I began to study the documents focusing on whether there might be any hope of Vanessa gaining full custody of Mandy. The divorce had been finalized slightly less than two years ago. The property division was straightforward. The couple was obviously financially well set. Vanessa got the five bedroom, three bath home located in Woodlawn, which I knew to be a gated community. Matt got the Porsche and Vanessa the Range Rover. Vanessa was required to sell the home no later than six months after Amanda turned eighteen, splitting the equity in the home with Matt. The couple divided equally their sizable investment accounts, retirement accounts, and other listed assets. Matt had to pay off all of the credit card bills which were not insignificant. Additionally, Matt was paying child support to the tune of $3500 a month, as well as Amanda's tuition for private schooling. Vanessa was receiving $2,500 in spousal maintenance, commonly known as alimony. Financially, Vanessa appeared to have made out quite well.

"Once custody is formally granted and the parameters for visitation are set, the law favors maintaining the court orders in effect," I explained. "This is especially true after a full-blown divorce trial like you had. To convince a judge to now revise or amend the original custody order, it must be shown that there has developed a substantial change in circumstances since the entry of the original decree. This substantial change must be of a significant nature such as living conditions, employment, or something that would have a substantial impact upon the child," I concluded.

Vanessa responded, "You mean I can't get full custody just because he's been an asshole?"

"That depends," I answered, chuckling. "Is that a substantial change in circumstances?"

"Not really," she replied. "I have come to the conclusion that has always been the case. In fact, The Asshole is the nickname I've given him. I have to be careful not to use it in front of Mandy," she said, giggling.

"With little or no change in circumstances, you'll face an uphill battle in getting the divorce decree changed," I replied. "You may, however, get some traction if you can present unbiased evidence of his poor parenting. You would need to find witnesses such as teachers, medical providers, and friends willing to testify concerning the negative impact Matt's parenting is having on Amanda's wellbeing. For example, a teacher who can testify as to Amanda's unacceptable behavior or substandard schoolwork after visitation with her father would be helpful. Even then, it would be a difficult battle with no guarantees, and quite expensive. Do you think a threatening letter from your attorney to Matt would cause him to reform his undisciplined parenting?"

"I'm afraid he would just get pissed off and cut off child support or do something awful to make life more miserable for me. Every time I make a reasonable request of him, it just backfires on me," she lamented with a frown as the tears began to flow. I handed her my trusty box of Kleenex.

Although Vanessa's proctological description of her husband was amusing, the situation did underscore the potential for an absurd result. Let's assume Matt was insane at the time the original divorce decree was signed by the judge. Technically, Vanessa could not later get the custody order changed by demonstrating that Matt was now nuts because she would not have shown a substantial change in circumstances. Fortunately, there is such a thing as judicial interpretation and judicial discretion to avoid absurd results.

After several more minutes of listening to Vanessa heap insults upon her former husband, I explained to her that the legal fees would initially run somewhere in the $7,500 to $8,500 range, or more, if we were to take the custody issue to court and bring forth witnesses. Suddenly her tune changed.

"I'll give it further thought and let you know," Vanessa said as she slipped on her luxurious coat, shook my hand, and shut the door behind her. I immediately jotted down my billable time of 1.2 hours, the exact length of our meeting, and turned my attention to other matters.

My thoughts were interrupted by my secretary's voice on the intercom. "Vanessa says she needs to talk to you for thirty seconds," she advised just as Vanessa rushed into my office.

"I apologize for barging back into your office," Vanessa began. "But my key fob just got flushed down the toilet! And I'm afraid my divorce papers might have gone with it."

Vanessa extended her right arm showing me her soggy coat sleeve, soaked to above the elbow. "I am so embarrassed. I made a quick grab, but my key fob was gone before I could reach it. Is there any chance I left the papers with you? Please say yes!"

Quickly locating the copy of her divorce decree, I handed the papers to a visibly relieved Vanessa. "Wait a minute," I said. "Let me run a copy of your papers to place in your file just in case you decide to follow up. And I'll have the building custodian try to locate your key fob."

18

Double Trouble

One person with two drunk driving citations in one night? How is that possible, I wondered as I began to read the report describing the incidents submitted by Trooper Williston.

The trooper's report read as follows:

From my position on the shoulder of the road, I observed the suspect's vehicle weaving back and forth across the center line and then to the shoulder, traveling 15 m.p.h. in a 45-m.p.h. zone. I followed the suspect for 2 blocks and then pulled him over with my flashing lights. No siren necessary. I first requested the suspect provide his driver's license and vehicle registration which he handed to me. I then asked him to step outside his vehicle which he did. As the suspect exited his vehicle, I smelled the strong odor of intoxicants about his person. The suspect was unable to recite the alphabet past the letter g, and was slurring his words. He appeared clearly intoxicated so I did not put him through any additional field sobriety tests. I then arrested the suspect and transported him to the police station where he was given a breathalyzer test.

The night officer on duty at the police station, Officer Klumke, noted on the intake sheet:

Suspect smells of alcohol, has bloodshot eyes, staggers when he walks and slurs his speech. Suspect has apparently urinated in his pants, there being a large dark wet spot on the crotch of his pants.

The breathalyzer test results showed that the driver, Pete Girard, had a blood alcohol level of .16%, double the presumptive level for intoxication in the State of Washington. Drunk driving laws have gotten progressively tougher in recent times. Once the suspect registers more than .08% blood alcohol, he or she is presumed to be driving while under the influence of alcohol with virtually no room for rebuttal. The only possible defenses are that there was no probable cause for the stop or that the breathalyzer was not functioning properly, both of which are longshots. The deterrents to driving intoxicated are big fines, loss of license, dramatically increased cost of insurance, and of course, the embarrassment factor.

Rather than calling his attorney at 1:45 a.m., Pete Girard made his one phone call to his wife, Glenda, who was neither amused nor sympathetic. Mrs. Girard did not come to the police station but instead sent Pete's brother, Bob Girard, to the rescue.

Pete was issued a Driving Under the Influence citation, assigned a court date, and was released to the custody of brother, Bob Girard. Bob was instructed by the trooper that, under no circumstances, was Pete to do any more driving that night.

Ten blocks from the police station, Pete and Bob were stopped at a red light when Pete recognized the rear end of his blue Camaro parked just beyond the intersection on the right. Pete suggested to Bob that Bob follow him home so Pete could avoid returning for his car the next day. "Are you sure you are good to drive the ten blocks home?" Bob asked his brother.

Officer Klumke was surprised to see Pete Girard being led back into the police station no less than 20 minutes after being released. This time Trooper Moreland had Pete by the collar, having issued him his second Driving Under the Influence citation within a forty-five minute time span.

"Clearly a new Walla Walla County record!" proclaimed Officer Klumke to all within earshot. Brother Bob was nowhere to be seen.

Pete's blood alcohol level was slightly lower than he had registered previously, which made sense, since alcohol dissipates from the bloodstream at the rate of roughly .015% per hour over time. Pete spent what remained of the night in the drunk tank.

What to do as a prosecutor to bring justice to this set of facts? As to the second citation, it was obvious Pete was so drunk that he was in no condition to make a rational decision regarding his attempt at driving home after his first offense. The counter argument, of course, was if I determined not to hold Pete culpable for the second citation because of his drunken condition, then why hold him accountable for his first offense, since in both instances his decision making was impaired?

Carefully reviewing Washington's drunk driving laws, I came upon an obscure statute which seemed to address Bob's participation in his brother's fateful evening. The seldom used law provided that a person who aids or abets another person in driving under the influence of alcohol can be cited by law enforcement with the same fines and penalties that pertain to the actual driver of the vehicle.

Brother Bob thought there was a mistake when he received a summons in the mail requiring him to appear in court on the charge of Aiding and Abetting Driving Under the Influence of Alcohol. The summons directed Bob to appear in court on the same date as his brother, a week from the following Friday.

Bob and Pete hired the same attorney, Steve Lewis, with whom I had dealt on many prior occasions. "What can we work out here on my two brother clients, Bob and Pete Girard?" Lewis asked me on the phone. "Both are really decent guys. Good Christian church-going contributing members of our community. Both have coached youth sports, soccer and baseball. Admittedly, Pete had too much to drink last Friday night. Seems like overkill to charge Pete twice. Bob made a mistake in judgment to let Pete drive a second time. But to give him an Aiding and Abetting Drunk Driving citation with all the penalties associated with it? That seems painfully excessive. Hopefully we can work out a plea deal for both these gentlemen. The good news is that you don't have to worry about setting bad precedent with a plea deal as I doubt you will ever see this same situation again."

"That much is most likely true," I replied not wanting to give anything away at that point.

"Can we at least continue the hearing on these cases for a couple of weeks?" Steve asked. "My wife and I are flying to Puerto Vallarta for two weeks. Leave tomorrow, January 20th."

"Nice timing on your part." I replied, glancing out my window at the foot of snow on the ground. "You caught me in a good mood. I'll agree to continue both cases for three weeks. Use plenty of sunscreen and have a margarita on me," I concluded, setting aside the Girard files.

19

Ain't no Mountain High Enough ♫

As it had been more than a month since my appearance in front of the Supreme Court in Olympia, I was anxious to learn the fate of little Teddy Fleming. On top of my stack of mail that Monday morning was a large white envelope addressed to me with the return address: *Clerk of the Washington State Supreme Court.*

Recalling my image of a line of nine black crows perched on a telephone wire, I sliced open the envelope with my sharp bronze letter opener. "Be good to me Justice Pike," I mumbled aloud as I began to read.

The letter, short and to the point, read as follows:

In re The Welfare of Theodore Barton Fleming: The decision of the trial court is hereby affirmed. Concerning the minor child, Theodore Barton Fleming, the parental rights of the mother, Wanda S. Fleming, and the child's unknown father are hereby terminated by Order of the Washington State Supreme Court.

"Yes!" I yelled at the wall in front of me. "The system worked!"

Next, I phoned Margaret Shafer, the caseworker who had monitored the situation from the time Teddy was a newborn.

"Good news in the Teddy Fleming case," I began. "I just received word that the Supreme Court upheld the trial court. It's official! Wanda's parental rights have now been fully terminated."

"That is such great news!" Margaret exclaimed. "Bill and Norma Robinson will be thrilled. They didn't want to get their hopes up but they did ask me for the name of an attorney who does adoptions. My guess is that once they receive the good news, they'll move quickly. You know, so many of these cases never seem to get anywhere. I can feel really good about this one.

Thanks for all you've done. Do you want to call the Robinsons and let them know?" she asked.

"You get that honor," I replied. "You were in on this from day one."

20

Bound For Bellingham

Another traffic court had just wrapped up late Friday afternoon when Detective Adams waved me aside. "Want to know the latest on our friend Winston Westerweller?" he asked. Detective Adams was all business, as usual.

"My best guess is he got caught stealing something again," I replied.

"No. Not this time. But about a week ago, he got beat up behind The Pastime Café. Got hit over the head with a rock or some other large blunt object.

They found him unconscious in the back alley. No suspects."

"Winston's head seems to be a popular target," I replied in a futile attempt to inject a little humor into the discussion.

Not a hint of a smile from the detective as he continued. "Winston spent two days in the hospital recovering. Now, here's where it gets really strange. Just before he left town, I saw him walking down Main Street dressed all in black, head to toe. Black baseball cap, black t-shirt, black pants and black tennis shoes. My sources tell me Winston was last seen boarding a bus bound for Bellingham."

"I'm guessing he'll find a job right away building boats. I hear business is booming," I replied. But the detective was already long gone, having chosen to ignore my breezy banter.

21
Family Planning

Signed into law by Abraham Lincoln in the midst of the Civil War, The Homestead Act of 1862 proved to be highly effective in expediting the development of the large expanse of western federal lands. After homesteading 160 acres of fertile farmland in the Walla Walla Valley from 1872 to 1877 for the requisite five years as required by The Homestead Act, George Jarstad received full title to the land from the United States government. Over the next twenty- five years, George purchased adjacent farmland so that he and his wife, Beulah, came to own a total of 640 acres, a full section. Two generations later, the land is now owned jointly by Seth and Wilbur Jarstad, grandsons of George and Beulah. Seth and Wilbur have been farming the land together for more than fifty years.

Seth, age 91, was seated across from me still wearing his faded red Con Agra Farms baseball cap over his tanned and wrinkled face. Squinting at me through thick frameless glasses, Seth proudly confirmed that he had driven his own car to my office, which caused me to wonder how many cars had to swerve off the road to avoid him.

Two years ago, shortly after Seth's wife Larita died, I had prepared a new will for him. Seth, who had lived through the Great Depression, complained bitterly about my bill of five hundred dollars which was at the extreme low end for the legal work involved. Nevertheless, I reduced the bill to three hundred dollars to keep the peace, while rationalizing that since Seth was worth several million, I would make it up in a few years when I probated his estate.

Forgetting for the moment that his attorney charged by the hour, Seth launched into a story about his days as a crop duster pilot. While crop dusting early one sunny summer morning, he was forced to make an emergency landing onto a plowed dirt field. As it turned out, the plane had run out of gas. Coincidentally, that would be a good way to describe Seth at this point in his life cycle.

"I swallowed a lot of dirt that day bringing her down in the field but managed to walk away unscathed," he proclaimed proudly. "Did jam my knee pretty good. The knee still bothers me now and then, but only if it's raining," he grinned. After chuckling about his near-death experience, Seth removed his glasses, reached into his pants pocket and pulled out a white cloth handkerchief. He proceeded to ceremoniously blow his nose, honking like a cornered goose. Wiping his eyes with his handkerchief, he replaced his glasses.

Now staring at me, he finally began, "The real reason I'm here is I think Wilbur and me need to divide up the farmland so his side of the family ends up with half, and my family, with the other half. Both our wives have passed. We aren't going to live forever. If we continue to leave it the way it is, our seven children will end up owning the land together. That is asking for serious trouble."

"Why is that a problem?" I asked, already guessing the answer. When land is owned by several family members, it is quite common for disputes to arise when decisions need to be made.

"Wilbur has four kids and I have three." He paused, and then added with a frown, "And judging from what just happened at Thanksgiving dinner, our kids won't be able to talk to each other let alone make farming decisions together."

"Tell me what happened during Thanksgiving dinner."

"Well," Seth responded, "the whole family was seated at the dining room table at my daughter Sylvia's place. We were all set to enjoy the turkey dinner when someone mentioned the name Trump. Then all hell broke loose. My niece, Olivia, stormed out of the house grabbing her bowl of mashed potatoes as she departed. She forgot the gravy, though. Lots of leftover gravy."

Pushing up his sweat stained red hat, Seth unfolded a crumpled piece of yellowed paper which proved to be a map of the family farmland. Pointing at the map with a bent arthritic index finger, he explained. "Our rectangular piece of land, 640 acres, should divide nicely between the north and south halves. Wilbur gets half and I get half. Then our kids don't have to deal with their cousins." His voice got noticeably quieter. "Just between you and me," he whispered conspiratorially, "I would like the south half. Much better farm ground."

Doing some quick mental math, I computed that the fertile 640 acres of wheat land, at a value of approximately $5,000 an acre, was worth somewhere in the neighborhood of $3.2 million dollars. "I may have a solution to your problem," I said. "Let's assume you want to end up with the south half. We can have both the south half and the north half separately valued by an appraiser. Then you pay Wilbur the difference in values to equalize. For example, if the south half is appraised at $2 mil and the north half at $1.2 mil, then you would pay Wilbur $400,000 to square up with him. Does that make sense? You would then own the south half as your separate property and could leave it to your three children free and clear. No cousins dealing with each other."

"How much will the appraisal cost me?" Seth asked with a frown.

"The appraisal would probably run you guys somewhere in the neighborhood of $4,500 to $6,000, but the appraisal would have other uses as well, such as for valuation purposes down the road for your estates. We'll also need to hire a professional surveyor to complete a survey to provide the correct legal descriptions so I can prepare the deeds each of you will need to sign to complete the process. When the dust settles, you will each own your respective 320 acres individually as your separate property."

Seth wrung his hands and squinted at me. After a pause, he replied, "Way too complicated. And it would cost way too much money to hire an appraiser and all the other stuff you mentioned. And no guarantee Wilbur would agree to give up the south half on that basis anyway."

There was another lengthy pause and a sigh from Seth. Then his eyes lit up. "How about we save time and a bunch of expense? A simple coin toss. Winner picks whichever half he wants. No money changes hands. We don't even get into values. Each of us ends up with 320 acres and we are done," he concluded triumphantly.

Seth gave me a concerned look and inquired, "Would you mind turning your meter off for just a moment? I need to use the bathroom."

"No problem," I replied. "Take all the time you need." Seth pushed himself up from the conference table and slowly trudged out of my office, closing the door behind him. Not more than thirty seconds had passed when Seth stuck his head back in the door. "Number two!" he announced and then disappeared again.

At first I didn't comprehend why Seth had added this additional disclosure. Then it sunk in. It was Seth's way of pointing out that he would be gone longer than I might have anticipated. This is way too much entertainment for me to charge this old guy my usual hourly rate, I thought.

Five minutes later, a more relaxed Seth was once again seated at the table across from me. "Let's pursue my coin toss idea."

"Here's the problem with a coin toss," I replied. "If the south half is worth far more than the north, then someone is going to get the short end of the stick. It could mean a difference of several hundred thousand dollars in relative values of the property each of you receives."

After some back and forth, it became clear that Seth was set on his coin toss idea. "If Wilbur agrees to it and he is competent, I see no legal reason why we can't go forward with a coin toss." I concluded. "But we need to make sure the result is not susceptible to being overturned down the road by any family member. I strongly suggest that before the coin toss takes place, you each sign a formal statement confirming you understand someone is going to lose out using this format. I also will need a letter from each of your physicians that confirms you are both competent. Wilbur should have his own attorney advising him or at least sign a statement that he was advised to get his own attorney."

"Wilbur is sharp as a tack. I'll tell him to get a letter from his doc. Let's get this little project going." Seth stated, clearly pleased that his cost saving plan was coming together.

"I'll put you and Wilbur on my schedule for a week from this Thursday at 10:00 am. We'll discuss the coin toss and see what he's thinking."

"Works for me. I'll get Wilbur in here. Probably a good idea if you have your secretary give each of us a reminder call the day before and also have her remind us to bring in those letters from our doctors, if you would please. I'll give her our phone numbers on my way out."

Seth had another thought. "I'm pretty sure Wilbur will agree that we need to divide it up, but what if he refuses? Am I stuck with him as my partner 'til one of us dies and all of our kids inherit?"

"We'll cross that bridge when we come to it," I replied, avoiding a complicated explanation of the procedure known in legal parlance as a partition action. A partition proceeding in court is the last resort when co-owners of real property cannot agree between themselves how their land is to be divided. If the land is not susceptible to division between the owners, a judge may order the land sold if one partner is unwilling or unable to buy out the other.

"How much is this going to cost me in legal fees and such?" he asked. "You know how much I like to spend money," Seth chuckled as he limped out of my office.

22

Phyllis Got It Right

Beatrice Elkins was back in my office, solo this time. No sign of her neighbor, Phyllis Boros, who had surreptitiously advised me, "She's loaded."

Once again Bea was talking about my dad. "My husband Harold and I bowled in the V.A. league with your mom and dad. Loved 'em both. Harold was a big San Francisco Giants fan as was your dad. They would talk endlessly about how the Giants were doing. I've always been a fan of the Giants too."

My childhood memories of time spent with my dad who had passed several years ago began flooding back as I responded to Phyllis' comments. "My dad and mom both grew up in Beacon, New York, sixty miles north of New York City on the Hudson River, right across the river from West Point. Dad went to college in New York City and then to N.Y.U. medical school. He began practicing medicine in New York in the late 1930s before the advent of antibiotics. He loved sports, and as a kid, became a diehard New York Giants baseball fan, attending ballgames at the Polo Grounds."

Now I was rolling and Bea was my captive audience. "Before the Giants moved to San Francisco, when I was just a little guy, Dad took me to the Polo Grounds in New York to watch the Giants play the St. Louis Cardinals. I remember watching my childhood hero, Willie Mays, patrolling centerfield while making his famous basket catches," I said as I pulled out my Willie Mays autographed baseball from the bottom drawer of my desk. "Dad also took me to watch a double header in Yankee Stadium the year Mickey Mantle and Roger Maris had their home run battle in 1961."

Realizing I had been reminiscing too long, I apologized. "Sorry I got a little nostalgic there. But I need to reassure you that you most definitely will not be billed for the time we spend chatting. Now I suggest we get down to business."

Together, Bea and I reviewed her handwritten list of assets that she had scrawled with a blue fountain pen on her lined notebook paper. She listed several substantial savings accounts, a six-figure certificate of deposit, and a home valued at $1.2 million. She also provided me with a recent investment account statement from her Morgan Stanley Wealth Management Advisor, Shannon Stafford, showing stocks and bonds worth just north of $4 million. Among the stocks in her investment account were one thousand shares of Microsoft.

"Harold bought those Microsoft shares back in 1986 when they first went public. He told me and everybody else many times that he bought the stock for $28 per share. Since he died, I have not paid much attention to it. Wonder what it is selling for today," she mused. "I suppose I should ask Shannon that question,"

"Just a second," I replied as I brought up Microsoft stock on my computer screen under the ticker symbol MSFT. "The current stock price of Microsoft is $425 per share," I announced. Then I scrolled down the page on my computer to COMPANY HISTORY. "It says here that the company went public in 1986 with the initial offering at $21 per share. But since then, the stock has split nine times. What an incredible investment! Harold was a smart man," I concluded.

"I had no idea till I wrote all this down that I was worth this much," Beatrice said incredulously. "Shannon has done a fabulous job for me."

"She's done such a good job that you will never be able to spend it all," I advised. "You should consider making some gifts to your children and grandchildren to avoid Washington inheritance tax. Twenty-six states impose an inheritance tax on their residents when they pass away. Each state is a little different. Washington State's inheritance tax begins on estates exceeding $2.2 million. Oregon starts at $1 million. New York begins their inheritance tax at $6.5 million. California and Arizona have no inheritance tax. Also everyone in the United States is subject to the federal estate tax. However, you don't have to worry about the federal estate tax because it does not kick in until an estate is much larger than yours."

"Wouldn't I have to pay a gift tax?" she asked.

"No gift tax in Washington and no gift tax due the federal government because your estate is well below the federal threshold for gift taxes."

I could see Beatrice's eyes glazing over. Too much information. I tried a different approach. "If you would like to pursue setting up a gifting plan for your children to avoid state inheritance tax, I'll work with your financial advisor. Together we can select the appropriate assets for gifting to your children and go from there. But you'll need to give Shannon authority to talk to me."

"Sounds good to me. I'll call Shannon as soon as I get home."

After Beatrice departed, in my best imitation of Phyllis' raspy smoker's voice, I announced to the walls of my empty office, "She's loaded!"

My next appointment was with John and Andrea Alston, the bimbo clause clients who were coming back to review the drafts of their wills. I began reviewing the Alston file to reacquaint myself with the documents so that I would be ready to address any questions they might have. Just then, my secretary buzzed in on the intercom.

"I just got a call from Andrea Alston. You know, that lady who wanted a bimbo clause. They're not going to make it in today. Says she is filing for divorce."

"Oh boy! Not good! But probably more effective than a bimbo clause in their wills," I replied.

I had my doubts that I would ever get paid for preparing the Alstons' complicated wills that were rendered irrelevant before they were signed. But there was a silver lining. I now was fully conversant with the term "bimbo clause."

23
The Plea Deal

Steve Lewis was on the phone. "How was Puerto Vallarta?" I asked the Girard brothers' attorney.

"We had a great time, but I was hoping the snow would be gone when we got back. My sunburn looks a bit out of place today. Now about the brothers and all their drunk driving charges. Can we come up with something that fairly addresses the situation? Admittedly, they both made bad decisions, but these are two really good guys who deserve a break. I might have mentioned that Pete is a Little League coach and Bob is president of Exchange Club. Pete is a realtor and Bob is a banker. Both men are active contributing members of our community. Neither has a criminal record of any sort."

After much back and forth with Lewis before the scheduled trial date, we reached a plea agreement as to both defendants. It wasn't perfect, but I felt it came close to fairly addressing this singularly unique set of facts. Pete Girard would plead guilty to the first drunk driving citation upon my dismissal of the second. His penalties were significant. Pete would lose his license for six months, be required to complete an alcohol education course, and pay a large fine, all of which were mandatory penalties under the law. Additionally, his car insurance premiums would skyrocket. And lastly, while Pete's driver's license was suspended for the next six months, Glenda would be his designated driver, a penalty I suspected would be far more painful than any punishment a court had the power to impose.

Brother Bob pleaded guilty to Aiding and Abetting Drunk Driving, but I agreed to hold his plea in abeyance for one year. If during the ensuing year Bob kept his nose clean, I would dismiss the charges against him, thus allowing him the possibility of avoiding the penalties. I was confident that Bob had learned his lesson.

In addition to all the penalties imposed by law, there were the substantial legal fees the Girard brothers had incurred with attorney Lewis who had successfully brokered a favorable plea deal with the tough deputy prosecuting attorney. And all things considered, two weeks at a fancy resort in Puerto Vallarta was not cheap.

At the conclusion of their guilty pleas, Pete Girard left the courtroom by way of the back entrance while Bob exited through the side door. Clearly the bonds of brotherhood had frayed a bit during their ordeal.

Post Script: If Pete Girard had killed a pedestrian after imbibing at his favorite local tavern, could the tavern be held liable for the wrongful death of the pedestrian? Dram Shop laws which establish legal responsibility for bars and restaurants who knowingly provide alcohol to obviously intoxicated persons vary from state to state. Accordingly, in some states there would be a viable lawsuit against the tavern owner, but not in all.

As to a private party host, if it can be shown that the host continued to serve his/her guest alcohol after the guest was noticeably intoxicated, the host may be held liable for damages to a third-party victim. The evidence that the guest was already intoxicated when the host continued to serve him/her must be substantial, however.

24

An Awesome Attorney

"I'm so happy to have all my estate planning stuff completed and I'm very pleased with the way it turned out," Beatrice Elkins said to me after she had signed her will in front of two witnesses, secretaries from my office. At my suggestion, Bea's will left her home exclusively to her two daughters while the remainder of her assets would pass in equal shares to all three children.

I had worked with Bea's Investment Advisor, Shannon Stafford, to develop a plan for Bea to begin making annual gifts from her investment account to her children and grandchildren to reduce her estate exposure to Washington inheritance tax. During this process, I had become acquainted with Bea's three children while obtaining their social security numbers needed to complete the gifts.

Whenever testamentary bequests to children were unequal, it had become my practice to encourage clients to provide a written explanation of their thinking at the same time they made out their wills. With the objective of maintaining harmony among my clients' heirs, I felt that providing full information to the kids would go a long way toward achieving that goal. Accordingly, I had prepared a separate letter for Bea's signature to be placed with her will. It read as follows:

To my children:

I am preparing this letter to my children to be placed with my will so my children will understand my thinking at the time I sign my will.

I want to first emphasize that I love all three of you equally. However, because I believe Bill has far more financial resources than Alice and Anita, after I am gone, my will provides that my home will pass exclusively to Alice and Anita. The remainder of my assets are to be distributed in equal shares to the three of you.

I trust that the three of you will always remain on good terms and be fully supportive of each other.

With love,

Beatrice (Mom)

"It's Alice Martin on line one for you," my secretary announced on the intercom. "She's Beatrice Elkins' daughter," she reminded me.

"I just wanted to tell you how pleased the entire family is with the estate planning you just completed for Mom," Alice gushed. "You are such an awesome attorney, getting Mom to start doing estate planning to avoid inheritance taxes!"

While I will take my compliments where I can get them, I suspected that Alice's enthusiasm for my work might have been slightly colored by the very substantial gift she had just received from her mother.

25

The Disney World Dad

Vanessa Vivalde was on my appointment calendar again today for 2:00 pm. As it had been several months since I last met with her, I reviewed Vanessa's file to reacquaint myself with the issues as well as the names of the protagonists. My notes were rather skimpy. The daughter's name was Amanda but Vanessa called her Mandy. The husband's name was Matt but Amanda referred to him as The Asshole. I chuckled at my notes.

I had also noted that Vanessa referred to Matt as the Disneyland Dad. Vanessa originally wanted full custody of Mandy but seemed to be less motivated when I quoted her the legal fees involved and explained the hurdles to surmount. I had explained that she would need to establish a substantial change in circumstances before a judge would consider modifying the existing divorce decree. Had Vanessa now decided to go forward with a custody battle?

Today Vanessa was dressed from head to toe in Lulu Lemon. "Just came from my yoga class," she announced as she bounced into my office. "You're not going to believe this," Vanessa began breathlessly. "Yesterday, Matt called to tell me that his company has given him a promotion. They are transferring him to the head office in Orlando, Florida. That's three thousand miles away!" she concluded triumphantly.

"So, do we now call him The Disney World Dad?" I asked.

"Nope. I'm sticking with The Asshole! He earned that nickname."

No longer able to resist, I took the bait. "How's that?"

My question caused Vanessa to launch into the lengthy history of Matt's misdeeds that led to his 'nom de guerre' and ultimately ended their marriage. First, she caught him cheating with a mutual female friend and told him to move out. Rather than divorcing, they tried marital counseling and began seeing a therapist once a week. Several months into their counseling, Matt had regained her trust and moved back into their home. Eight months later, while organizing their large walk-in closet, Vanessa came upon a crumpled Hilton Hotel receipt in the right rear pocket of Matt's slacks. When she did not recognize the credit card, she began sleuthing. Reviewing Matt's office credit card expenditures over the past six months, Vanessa found numerous charges for other hotel rooms, restaurants, flowers, and even jewelry.

Having concluded her tale of Matt's second fall from grace, Vanessa was back on the issue at hand, "So is this the substantial change in circumstances you said I needed to get full custody of Mandy?"

"Moving three thousand miles away should do the trick," I replied. "But I'm wondering. Did the subject of modifying Mandy's custody come up in your conversation with Matt?"

"I didn't want to deal with his anger, so I didn't even mention custody. I'm going to leave that up to you," she concluded with the slightest hint of a wry smile.

"O.K. Let's see who represented Matt during the divorce," I said thumbing through the divorce decree. Matt's attorney was Ernest Eichler, a local attorney who aggressively represented his clients, but was generally reasonable and a straight shooter.

I had several options concerning how to approach modifying the custody order. If Matt were still represented by legal counsel, then ethically I was required to communicate through his attorney. But arguably, Eichler's representation ended when the divorce was finalized so I could now elect to contact Matt directly by sending him a letter requesting a change in custody.

A more aggressive approach was to bypass preliminary communication with Matt altogether by immediately filing with the court a formal Motion for Change of Custody. I would then hire a process server to deliver the papers to Matt who would be granted ten days to respond. In my experience, however, serving legal documents by process server was not conducive to a cooperative resolution of the issues.

Instead, I opted for a less adversarial (and less expensive) approach. I called Ernie Eichler, Matt's attorney during the prior proceedings. Over the phone, I explained the situation to Ernie telling him I would be sending him a letter together with a proposed Agreed Order that would reflect Matt's move to Orlando. The Order would provide that

Vanessa would have sole custody while Matt would have reasonable visitation. There would be provisions for child support as well as other details. Ernie and I agreed to work together to avoid battling in court. Ernie thanked me for the call while indicating that once I delivered the paperwork to him, he would get Matt into his office to review the proposed modification and, thereafter, get back to me with a response.

While my hope was that Matt would continue to utilize Eichler, he also had choices regarding how to respond. He could change attorneys or choose to represent himself. He could fight the proposed change in custody tooth and nail, or work with us to come to a quick agreement that saved on attorney fees while avoiding the expense and stress of an extended legal battle.

Our proposed Agreed Order sent to Mr. Eichler called for Vanessa to have sole custody of Amanda because of changed circumstances. Alimony would remain at $2,500 per month. Child support would be increased to $5,000 per month since it was obvious Matt would be earning more because of his promotion. I requested Matt pay Vanessa's attorney fees associated with the custody modification. Additionally, our proposal called for Matt being granted visitation rights including alternate Christmas holidays, two weeks in the summer and phone calls at least once per week.

I knew Matt would not accept all the terms of our proposed Agreed Order but it was a starting point for negotiating purposes. "Let's just hope they don't fight the sole custody issue," I said to Vanessa as she approved the proposal set forth in my letter to Eichler. "I don't see how they can argue custody with Matt moving so far away. The rest is negotiable."

A few days later, I had Eichler's letter setting forth Matt's counterproposal which specified that Matt would receive six weeks visitation in the summer, visitation every Christmas holiday, copies of all report cards to Matt, each party to pay their own attorney fees, child support to remain at $3,500 per month, alimony at $2,500 per month, and unlimited contact with Amanda by phone. To my relief, there seemed to be acquiescence in granting Vanessa full custody which made sense given Matt would be three thousand miles away.

When I explained Matt's position to Vanessa, the tears began to flow. I had long ago learned the importance of keeping a box of Kleenex close by for just these situations. As Vanessa dabbed at her eyes with a Kleenex, I attempted to reassure her. "The good news is there seems to be no dispute with your being granted full custody which was your primary goal the first time you came into my office. Keep in mind, we are still in the negotiating phase of this process. Generally speaking, each side will give a little until we reach an agreement. If Matt remains unreasonable, then we'll let a judge decide."

"I understand," Vanessa replied, blowing her nose, wiping the tears from her eyes, as she regained her composure.

"So, let's look at their position and see where we might compromise to bring this to conclusion." I continued. Together, we mapped out a position Vanessa could live with if Matt would agree.

After two months of much back and forth between attorneys, and four additional appointments with Vanessa whose wardrobe was seemingly unlimited, we were able to reach a formal Agreement to modify the custody decree without court proceedings. Vanessa would gain full custody of Amanda. Matt would continue to pay $3500 per month in child support while each party would pay their own attorney fees. Matt would have Amanda with him each summer for one month and alternating years for

Thanksgiving and Christmas holidays. Vanessa would make Amanda available to talk with Matt on the phone at least once per week. Matt would pay all travel expenses for Amanda to visit him. The previous court orders regarding alimony and division of property would remain in full force and effect.

Vanessa was back in my office in good spirits to sign the negotiated Agreement. "Has The Asshole already signed?" she asked as I handed the papers to her.

"He signed it," I replied, by now fully comfortable with Matt's nickname. Vanessa signed the Agreement with a flourish.

Because both husband and wife had signed the Agreed Order changing custody, as had both their attorneys, it was now a mere formality for me to obtain the judge's signature approving the change in custody and other terms agreed upon. Essentially, my work was done.

"Congratulations on a good result without having to go to battle in court," I complimented Vanessa, "And now that I will no longer be working for you, I have a little gift for you," I announced as I handed Vanessa a 4-inch square dark blue velvet jewelry box.

"What is this?" she asked with a quizzical look on her face. "I didn't know lawyers gave their clients gifts as their cases were concluding."

"Just a little something I felt you should have to celebrate the successful resolution of your case. Go ahead and open it now."

"Oh my God," Vanessa exclaimed with a loud belly laugh. "It's my Range Rover key fob!"

26

All in the Family

I quickly learned that attorneys spend a lot of time just waiting outside courtrooms for their cases to be called. Monday was docket day when the court heard a variety of motions and other preliminary matters not requiring a full trial. The order in which various matters were brought before the court was set forth on the Monday docket sheet which the court clerk circulated among the attorneys so that they would have some idea when their case would be heard. Matters that were to take more than fifteen minutes were put at the bottom of the docket.

Although my case did not appear until the docket's fourth page, I never knew how fast prior matters would move along. Several cases ahead of me might be continued to a later date for one reason or another which meant my case could be called much sooner than anticipated. Conversely, I could spend half a day waiting for my case to be called as matters ahead of me dragged on before the judge. From the attorney's perspective (and the paying client), the Monday docket seemed well designed to create "a hurry up and wait" scenario.

On that particular Monday morning, I was seated on a wooden bench in the hallway outside the courtroom next to the judge's chambers waiting my turn to appear in court. I was there on a criminal arraignment for a defendant who was having his first court appearance before the judge. I had charged the defendant with possession of cocaine discovered during a routine traffic stop by a city police officer who had initially pulled the driver over because his left rear tail light was out. As the prosecutor, I would read the criminal charges against the defendant. The judge would then ask the defendant if he had an attorney. If he could not afford one, the judge would appoint an attorney for him at state expense. The defendant was required to sign an affidavit swearing to his financial need for a public defender.

Under the Sixth Amendment to The United States Constitution, the accused has a right to a speedy trial as well as the right to representation by legal counsel. In the State of Washington, a trial date must be set within ninety days of the first court appearance if the accused is not in jail, and within sixty days if the accused is held in jail. Since delay is sometimes the best tactic a defense attorney can bring to the table, the initial trial date is often continued to a later date, but only after the accused, based upon the advice of legal counsel, has signed a Waiver of Speedy Trial. Without the signed Waiver, there is a right to dismissal if the accused is not brought to trial within the confines of the speedy trial rule. As prosecutor, it was imperative that I be vigilant regarding obtaining a signed Waiver if the case were to be delayed beyond the speedy trial constraints mandated by the 6th Amendment.

I was killing time reviewing my text messages when I noticed Reggie Reser approaching from my left. He was walking side by side with an elegantly dressed middle-aged gentleman I presumed to be his client. As the twosome got closer, I took in Reggie's appearance. Sporting a light grey tailored suit, white dress shirt, and dark red tie, Reggie looked particularly put together that morning, especially compared to his western garb he had worn during our recent appearance before the Washington Supreme Court.

"Hey Reggie," I announced as he passed. "You look great in a suit!"

"Thanks," Reggie muttered under his breath while quickly moving past me without a second look.

"What was that all about?" I heard Reggie's client ask him as they passed out of earshot.

Suddenly to my left, the judge's large oak door burst open. Pouring out from the judge's chambers was the entire Robinson family, Bill, Norma and their two little girls. In the center of the group, beaming ear to ear, marched little Teddy, proudly holding onto the strings attached to five giant red balloons floating high above him.

"The adoption was just finalized in the judge's chambers," Norma Robinson gushed. "Theodore Barton Robinson is now a full-fledged member of our family!" she announced proudly to all within earshot.

A true high five, I thought, gazing up at the balloons drifting like a colorful canopy hovering above the celebrating family. As Teddy ran toward me, I dropped to one knee and gave him a big bear hug, celebrating the feel-good moment with the entire Robinson family.

27
The Quarterback

Ten a.m. Thursday morning as planned, both elderly Jarstad brothers were seated across from me at my conference table. Seth introduced me to brother Wilbur, who was sporting a red plaid flannel shirt and blue jeans held up by black suspenders. Wilbur was holding his blue and green sweat stained Seattle Mariners baseball cap in his left hand and squinting at me through frameless spectacles very similar to those worn by his older brother. With his hunched over frame and wrinkle webbed face, Wilbur reminded me of a tired wasp in October.

After some preliminary pleasantries, I got down to business. "Okay gentlemen. It is my understanding that you are considering dividing up your 640 acres of farmland so that each of you will end up owning 320 acres, individually. Once the land division is completed, you will each be in a position to fully control your half of the land and leave it separately to your children. The cousins will no longer have to deal with each other. Are you both in agreement as to the need to now divide the land?"

"That's what we need to do," Wilbur confirmed. "Can't have the seven cousins owning the land all together. You probably heard about the disaster at Thanksgiving dinner."

"We both agree to divide it up," Seth stated matter-of-factly. "Gotta split it in two."

I continued. "Seth has proposed a coin toss to decide who gets first choice of half the land, the south half or north half. Do you agree with that format?" I asked looking at Wilbur, "Even though there is most likely a significant difference in the value of the two halves?"

"Sounds fair to me," Wilbur stated. "I am in agreement with that approach."

"Here are the letters from our doctors you requested," Seth said, sliding two pieces of white paper across the conference table to me. "Both our docs say we still know what we're doin, believe it or not," he chuckled as I placed the doctors' letters in my file.

Next, I set forth the parameters for the coin toss about to take place. "The two of you are in agreement that we will flip a coin. Whoever wins gets his choice of the north half, which is 320 acres, or the south half, also 320 acres, whichever he wants without regard to the value of either half. I will then prepare the deeds. It is clear to both of you that no money will change hands between the two of you. In effect, we are disregarding the relative values of the north and south half. Is that agreed?" I asked, looking first at Wilbur and then to Seth.

"Agreed," Seth and Wilbur said in unison as Seth pulled out a shiny quarter from deep in the right pocket of his faded jeans.

I thought to add, "And you will both split equally the costs involved in this process including my legal fees, court filings etc." Both men grimaced at the thought of having to pay these expenses but gave me simultaneous nods.

Before the coin toss, I produced a brief written Agreement reflecting their understanding as to the format for dividing the land in half. The Agreement set forth all the points we had discussed concluding with the statement that no money would change hands even though the two halves might be of unequal value. Both men quickly reviewed and signed the written Agreement above their printed names. I placed the signed Agreement in the Jarstad file as a precaution against future complaints by family members regarding the land division.

"Ok. Gentlemen, the coin toss is on. Seth will flip the coin and Wilbur will call it, heads or tails," I announced authoritatively with the goal of moving this project along.

"I couldn't catch it," Seth said apologetically, squinting at me through his thick glasses.

"Me neither," added Wilbur who was in no better shape than his brother.

"Here, you flip it," Seth said to me, placing the shiny quarter in my right hand.

Now staring at the coin in my right palm, my mind began racing. I had no training in law school on how to play the role of The Coin Flipper. I paused. Recalling that before the opening kickoff of every football game I had ever watched there was a coin toss. I will just play the role of the football referee conducting the pre-game coin toss.

"Gentlemen," I began authoritatively, "I am showing you a quarter with a head on one side, that being the side featuring George Washington, and a tail on the other side, that being a depiction of the American eagle. "Who wants to call it?"

"Let Seth call it. He's the oldest," offered Wilbur.

"O.K. I'll call it," Seth responded.

"I will now flip the coin and Seth will call heads or tails," I announced with all the drama I could muster in the moment. "If Seth calls it correctly, he gets his choice of the north half or the south half of the 640 acres. If Seth calls it wrong, then Wilbur gets first choice. Agreed?"

"Agreed," both brothers said once again in unison.

Flipping the shiny quarter three feet in the air with my right thumb, it spun over and over reflecting the light with each turn before I deftly caught it in the palm of my right hand. I quickly placed the quarter on my left wrist while carefully covering the coin with my right hand. "Call it Seth," I said, still firmly concealing the coin.

Seth hesitated, then called out, "Tails!"

"Tails it is," I announced as I lifted my right hand off the coin, showing both gentlemen the American eagle. "It will be Seth's choice."

Seth looked at Wilbur who was expressionless and then looked at me. He scratched the few remaining gray hairs on his forehead, then began drumming his fingers on the table. "This is a tough one," he said, milking the moment. "I'm just not sure which one to pick." Finally, after thirty seconds of silence, in a soft voice barely above a whisper, Seth said, "I suppose I'll take the south half, although it's a difficult decision."

"Okay, it's settled," I announced. "I'll order the survey and prepare the deeds in accordance with the Agreement. It may take a week or two before the survey is completed. My secretary will give you a call when the deeds are ready for your signatures."

Neither brother smiled nor said a word as they departed my office, providing no hint as to how they felt about the outcome of the coin toss. As the two stooped gentlemen shuffled down the hallway, I closed my office door behind them.

Alone now, I pondered why Seth showed so much hesitancy before selecting the south half after previously confessing to me that he coveted that very parcel. Maybe something as simple as Seth feeling bad about getting the better of his brother to the tune of several hundred thousand dollars when considering the disparity in land values?

Or was it something much deeper than that? The division of the land did mark a monumental change in their lengthy and peaceful relationship. Decades and decades of sharing ownership of the farmland with all the decisions they made together through the years. What crops to plant and when to plant them every year? When to begin tilling the soil? Timing for fertilizer and spray? What equipment to purchase? Crop loans? Crop insurance? Going through harvests together. Whatever the underlying subtleties, dividing the land by the two elderly brothers was undeniably a wise decision to avoid future disputes among the seven contentious cousins.

Shifting gears, I began reviewing my morning mail. A local attorney had sent a letter concerning a recently completed bitter divorce battle involving child custody and visitation. He was inquiring as to whether my client would consider trading holiday visitations. Easter weekend for the 4th of July?'

Just then, there was a soft knock on my heavy oak door. It was Seth. No sign of brother Wilbur who had apparently left the building. Seth limped in slowly.

Was he going to explain his hesitancy in selecting the south half after winning the coin toss? Instead, he squinted at me through his thick rimless glasses, hesitated, and, tilting his head asked apologetically, "Would it be possible to get my quarter back?"

A Final Word from the Author

Having just closed the door to my law practice after forty-six years, I knew there was a book that was begging to be written. The real-life stories were just too entertaining to be placed in a filing cabinet and quickly forgotten. But writing a book is hard work and there were many distractions.

With no deadline for completion, I needed to find incentive to finish the project. After several months of spinning my wheels, I came up with a plan. I told everyone I knew that I was working on a book, placing pressure on myself to get going. Walla Walla is a small town and the word got around that I was writing a book. Wherever I went, there was always someone asking, "How's that book coming?" As the weeks stretched into months, and the months stretched into a couple of years, the question became, "Are you ever going to finish that book? I want a signed copy."

"Almost finished," I would reply, and back I would go to typing on my computer. Now I can finally say with equal measures of relief and pride, "I am finally done!"

While blood and guts crimes are dramatic and sensational, I determined, for my first book, to limit my storytelling to cases portraying the lighter side of my legal experience. It's not that I wasn't involved in a fair number of violent felonies during my four years in the Prosecutor's Office. I experienced a murder trial with multiple victims, a kidnapping and assault trial, as well as a fatal stabbing at a local steakhouse that led to murder charges. There were also several jury trials concerning escape, assault and murder at the Washington State Penitentiary. I am saving the violent crimes for my next book.

In hindsight, the Prosecutor's Office was the perfect launching pad for my legal career. While practicing law in the big city may have been more glamorous, I was fully content with the wide variety of legal challenges I faced daily in my small town law practice.

Every time we visited Seattle, it rained cats and dogs and the traffic was terrible. An eight minute commute to my office and a sunnier climate were not to be discounted in my over all assessment that settling in Walla Walla was the right decision.

Many thanks to family and friends for all their encouragement, suggestions, and, above all, their patience in bringing this effort to completion. The support I received was invaluable.

Made in United States
Troutdale, OR
11/03/2026

56852694R00120